THE STATE OF THE UNIVERSITY, 2000–2008

The State of the University, 2000–2008

Major Addresses by
UNC Chancellor James Moeser

James Moeser

FOREWORD BY JAMES L. LELOUDIS

Copyright © 2018 James Moeser. All rights reserved.

Suggested citation: Moeser, James. *The State of the University, 2000-2008: Major Addresses by UNC Chancellor James Moeser.* Chapel Hill: Institute for the Arts & Humanities at the University of North Carolina at Chapel Hill, 2018. doi: https://doi.org/10.5149/9781469641232_Moeser

Cover image: Portrait of James Moeser by John Howard Sanden. Used with permission of the artist.

ISBN 978-1-4696-4121-8 (hardcover)
ISBN 978-1-4696-4768-5 (pbk: alk. paper)
ISBN 978-1-4696-4122-5 (ebook)

Published by the Institute for the Arts & Humanities, University of North Carolina at Chapel Hill

Distributed by the University of North Carolina Press
www.uncpress.org

To Susan, my love and my rock.

CONTENTS

Acknowledgments • ix

Foreword, James L. Leloudis • xi

Introduction, James Moeser • xv

CHANCELLOR JAMES MOESER'S
INSTALLATION REMARKS
The University of North Carolina at
Chapel Hill, October 12, 2000 • 1

2001 STATE OF THE UNIVERSITY ADDRESS
The University of North Carolina at
Chapel Hill, September 5, 2001 • 11

A TEMPEST IN A TEXTBOOK: ACADEMIC
FREEDOM AND THE QUR'AN CONTROVERSY
Remarks to the National Press Club,
Washington, D.C., August 27, 2002 • 27

2002 STATE OF THE UNIVERSITY ADDRESS
The University of North Carolina at
Chapel Hill, September 4, 2002 • 33

2003 STATE OF THE UNIVERSITY ADDRESS
The University of North Carolina at
Chapel Hill, October 12, 2003 • 49

2004 STATE OF THE UNIVERSITY ADDRESS
The University of North Carolina at
Chapel Hill, September 29, 2004 • 63

2005 STATE OF THE UNIVERSITY ADDRESS
The University of North Carolina at
Chapel Hill, September 15, 2005 • 77

2006 STATE OF THE UNIVERSITY ADDRESS
The University of North Carolina at
Chapel Hill, September 12, 2006 • 91

2007 STATE OF THE UNIVERSITY ADDRESS
The University of North Carolina at
Chapel Hill, September 26, 2007 • 105

THE TASK FOR LEADERSHIP:
SUSTAINING RESEARCH EXCELLENCE
IN UNCERTAIN TIMES
Remarks for the Merrill Center Research
Conference, The University of Kansas,
July 21, 2010 • 121

REMARKS FOR THE UNVEILING
OF THE PORTRAIT
The University of North Carolina at
Chapel Hill, October 7, 2011 • 137

ACKNOWLEDGMENTS

I am indebted to the loyal support and editing of Nancy Davis, Mike McFarland, and Cecilia Moore, who provided enormous assistance in the preparation of these addresses at the time of their delivery, and to Tatjana Zimbelius-Klem, William Kumpf, and Melissa Clay who edited them for publication.

I am particularly indebted to the staff of the Institute for the Arts and Humanities who assisted in the preparation of the text as well as liaison with UNC Press: Tommie Watson, Rebecca Williams, Allison Burnett Smith, and Hannah Perez.

Additional support came from the College of Arts and Sciences, and I am deeply indebted to Dean Kevin Guskiewicz and Senior Associate Dean Terry Rhodes.

FOREWORD

The university, James Moeser writes, is above all else "a vale of soul-making." It is a free, creative space where we seek new knowledge to resolve the great troubles of our world; a stage on which we celebrate beauty, art, and the shared humanity that transcends our differences; and above all else, a sanctuary of learning where students set the course for life's journey. That is the vision that Moeser brought to the University of North Carolina at Chapel Hill, and to American higher education more broadly, during his eight-year tenure as chancellor. It is laid out here in his annual State of the University addresses and other key speeches, collected for the first time in a single volume.

James Moeser arrived in Chapel Hill in the summer of 2000, at what he calls a "precipitous moment" in the university's history. Carolina was "highly ranked, but also highly vulnerable." State lawmakers had made a series of deep cuts in the university's budget, years of deferred maintenance had left the campus ragged around the edges, and private peers were using their immense endowments to poach faculty with alarming success. In short, the leadership challenge was daunting.

Moeser responded with a simple but high-risk strategy: set audacious goals and leverage resources aggressively. One point of hope was the bond referendum that was on the November ballot that year. It promised $3.1 billion to improve higher education facilities statewide, roughly half a billion of which was earmarked for the Chapel Hill campus. In his installation address, delivered just a month before Election Day, Moeser seized the political opportunity and pledged that he would raise private support to match public investment three-dollars-to-one. Weeks later, the bond referendum passed in all 100 North Carolina counties. That outcome was a resounding affirmation of voters' faith in the university.

Success at the ballot box added momentum to the university's Carolina First capital campaign, which had been launched in 1999 with a $1.8 billion goal. Over the next eight years, the campaign roared past that target with a final tally of $2.38 billion. New public and private resources fueled a building boom that at times seemed to transform the entire campus into a construction site. People joked that students would graduate with a belief that the school colors had been changed to the orange and white of safety fences, and that the letters "U-N-C" stood for University of Never-Ending Construction. The Carolina First campaign also provided new resources for faculty salaries, graduate stipends, and undergraduate scholarships. On all fronts, the university strengthened its competitive edge in recruiting—and in the case of faculty, retaining—top talent.

The infusion of capital and new state-of-the-art infrastructure helped to fuel a remarkable advance in research productivity. In 2000, external peer-reviewed research funding totaled $375 million; from there, it marched steadily upward to top $1 billion in 2016. But there was more than money, bricks, and mortar behind that achievement. It was also driven by a campus culture that Moeser describes as the university's "secret weapon." Visitors often sense a spirit here that is difficult to name. I think of it as a culture of humility and collaboration. Moeser describes it as a "strong tradition of working together across departmental and divisional lines and not caring who gets the credit." It is a recognition that few great ideas spring fully formed from an individual mind. They arise instead from shared curiosity and an open exchange of discoveries. In our hypercompetitive and highly individualistic society, such an ethos is to be treasured. It is the very lifeblood of creativity and innovation.

Amid all of these changes, Carolina might easily have lost sight of its public mission. Budget cuts continued, with only episodic relief, at public institutions nationwide; tuition increases followed with inexorable regularity, setting the stage for what has become a full-blown student debt crisis that threatens access to college; and policy makers were abandoning a post-WWII consensus on support for public universities as an essential social investment. On every front, Americans were treating higher education more as a private than a public good. In Chapel Hill, Moeser and his leadership team bucked that trend, and they did so flamboyantly. In 2004, the university established the Carolina Covenant, a program that uses scholarships, grants, and work-study employment to guarantee debt-free education for undergraduate students whose family earnings fall below 200 percent of the federal poverty line. The program reached back in time to tap a defining element of the university's history, when for generations it opened a door of opportunity in what was otherwise a desperately poor state. Today, 15 percent of Carolina undergraduates are Covenant Scholars, and one in five is a first-generation student. Those are poignant measures of what it means to be a truly *public* university.

The Carolina Covenant speaks to the university's core values, what Moeser calls its strong "moral compass." In each of his State of the University speeches, he challenged us to keep those values front-of-mind and to reflect on their meaning for our research, teaching, and public service. He reminded us that in the early 20th century Carolina rose to prominence as a world-class institution on the basis of its "courage and fortitude" in confronting the ills of regional and national life: racism, poverty, injustice, sickness, and illiteracy. That fortitude was often tested, and the university sometimes failed terribly in living up to its ideals.

But Carolina shone in the fall of 2002 as the campus prepared for discussion of a book on the Qur'an that had been selected as a reading assignment for incoming first year students. Just days before the semester opened, critics complained that the university was choosing sides in what they characterized as a clash of civilizations ignited by the 9/11 terrorist attacks. They filed suit in federal court, challenged the university's budget in the legislature, and questioned academic freedom in the statewide university system's board of governors. I was in London at the time and heard the news on the BBC. It was a big deal; the world was watching.

The summer reading program survived, but in the time since the Qur'an controversy the underlying disagreements have only intensified. They led most recently to decisions by the board of governors to shut down the university's Center on Work, Poverty, and Opportunity, as well as its Center on Civil Rights—both housed in the School of Law. A majority on the board argued that the centers had strayed from the university's educational mission into advocacy. That charge stands in sharp contrast to Moeser's notion that the university has a "moral responsibility" to engage critical social issues and "make the world a better place." The conflict is unlikely ever to be fully resolved, because as Moeser notes, it is grounded in a tension fundamental to our historical conception of higher education as "both a conservator of culture and values and a leader of change."

Like university executives across the nation, Moeser steered through difficult times by reminding policy makers and the public that great flagship institutions are engines of economic development and job creation. And when necessary, he called on a political action committee made up of well-connected alumni to drive the message home. Moeser also understood the danger of overplaying that hand—of undermining the university's core strengths in the arts and humanities, which would never pay dividends close to those of the sciences and health care disciplines. The university, he insisted, has a responsibility to attend to our souls as well as our wallets.

Moeser underscored that principle with a major new arts initiative. When he arrived in Chapel Hill, the university's arts infrastructure was embarrassingly inadequate. Performance spaces were showing their age; some were threadbare and still lacked air conditioning. In almost every case, they belied the underlying academic distinction of faculty and students in the arts disciplines. Moeser addressed those deficiencies by announcing an $11 million renovation of Memorial Hall, the university's main arts venue, and by making a major investment in an initiative called Carolina Performing Arts. The transformation that followed was inspiring and intellectually invigorating. Carolina Performing Arts made the Memorial Hall stage a coveted destination for world-class dancers and musicians. Those visitors captivated us with puppetry from West Africa and Indonesia, they taught us about the Sufi tradition in Islam, schooled us in the poetry of urban hip-hop and rap, and introduced us anew to the artistic traditions of Europe and North America. In a world in which we too often seek to discover only what we already know, Carolina Performing Arts has shown how the university might serve as "a true model of a multicultural, pluralistic society."

There is wisdom in these pages, along with sober reflection on the current state of American higher education. This volume will stir the hearts of loyal Tar Heels and provoke thoughtful reflection by all who appreciate the unique contributions a public university can make to the project of building and sustaining a just, inclusive, and democratic society.

James Leloudis
Professor of History
Peter T. Grauer Associate Dean for Honors Carolina
Director, The James M. Johnston Center for Undergraduate Excellence
College of Arts and Sciences

INTRODUCTION

One of my most important personal disciplines as Chancellor of the University of North Carolina at Chapel Hill from 2000–2008 was the annual State of the University Address. I use the word discipline quite literally: it was the process I used to organize my thoughts and to formulate my own agenda for myself and for the University. These addresses, always delivered at the beginning of the academic year, were my means of inspiring the faculty, staff, and students to have a sense of pride and purpose.

Most of my public utterances as Chancellor were crafted by other people: speech writers on staff, whose work I depended on for the very frequent public appearances a Chancellor must make—sometimes several times a day. Not so the State of the University Address. I wrote these speeches myself, spending weeks in the preparation of these addresses, writing material that would—without editing—have taken hours to deliver. That is where my excellent staff came to my rescue, helping me to pare down the remarks to what was essential to say and helping me craft a text that was, I hope, elegant and powerful.

There is a pastoral element to university leadership. As a young boy, I used to imagine delivering sermons from a great high pulpit. I thought about becoming a minister, but clearly, God did not call me to that vocation. These addresses, however, were my sermons to the University—intended to inspire, motivate, and instill a sense of mission in our faculty, staff, and students.

I have presented these addresses in chronological order, beginning with my Installation Address on University Day, Oct. 12, 2000. That was an exciting moment for me, and I believe for Carolina as well. The campus was still in shock from the sudden death of Chancellor Michael Hooker a year before. The campus was physically crumbling, after years of deferred maintenance and little new construction, but it was eagerly anticipating the passage of the higher education bond issue on the November 2000 ballot, what is still today the largest higher education construction bond ever passed by any state.

I have omitted only the personal introductions and references to individuals, the "bread and butter recognitions," at the beginnings of each address. Otherwise, they are just as delivered.

THE STATE OF THE UNIVERSITY, 2000–2008

CHANCELLOR JAMES MOESER'S
INSTALLATION REMARKS

The University of North Carolina at Chapel Hill
October 12, 2000

AN OLD PROVERB SAYS, "We drink from wells that we did not dig, and we are warmed by fires that we did not build."

On my first day on the job, I did what countless Carolina students have been doing for years for good luck on the first day of class—I took a drink from the Old Well. So today, I take another drink of that water—to cool my own voice for these remarks, but also to draw from the well of history as we lay out the vision for Carolina's future. With the smiling face of providence and hard work by all of us, we stand at the precipice of a new golden age for Carolina, a 21st century Renaissance.

Our Founding Fathers knew what they were doing when they planted the seeds for a new kind of university in America, realizing that a radical experiment in democracy required an enlightened electorate. Thomas Jefferson wrote, "The God who gave us life, gave us liberty at the same time." The framers of our republic realized that liberty and democracy were fragile, that the old order of education only for a hereditary aristocracy would provide an insufficient foundation for building a republic.

Thus, North Carolinians, under the leadership of William Richardson Davie, on this very day in 1793 established the nation's first public university to be the wellspring of freedom, the light on the hill of liberty, with its motto "Lux, Libertas"—"Light and Liberty."

In that moment, in Chapel Hill, American public higher education was born. It has fallen to a succession of generations to keep Chapel Hill's flame of enlightenment rekindled and the well of liberty replenished.

Critical Defining Moments

Since my appointment last April, I have immersed myself in the history of this great institution. What stands out most vividly is the degree to which we have experienced several critical defining moments—points in time where the university took great strides that changed its culture or character by orders of magnitude.

Certainly, the foundation in 1793 was such a moment. So was the second opening of Chapel Hill in the aftermath of the Civil War and Reconstruction. One woman's tenacity—that of Cornelia Phillips Spencer—kept the flame of light and liberty alive. Her remarkable campaign, marked by newspaper columns and visits to key state leaders, resulted finally in an appropriation from a destitute state. In 1875, on the day word came from Raleigh of the General Assembly's action, she climbed the stairs of South Building and rang the bell, signaling that this mighty university would not die.

In his inaugural address in 1915, President Edward Kidder Graham opened a great new chapter in our history, declaring that the university is the "instrument of democracy" for realizing the state's aspirations. Graham linked the University's work with good roads, public health, city and county planning, rural economics, sociology, and civic problems.

During this period, the university received the bequest of Mary Lily Kenan Flagler, one of the largest such gifts ever made to a state university at that time, creating the Kenan Professorships. Three decades later John Motley Morehead established the Morehead Scholarships. These gifts lifted North Carolina above the status of a good regional university, helping it become a great national university for the people of North Carolina.

To read the history of this place is to study the giants who bestrode it—Kemp Battle, Francis Preston Venable, Edward Kidder Graham, Harry Woodburn Chase, Frank Porter Graham, and two modern giants who are still with us, presidents emeriti Bill Friday and C.D. Spangler, Jr.

I am blessed that four of my predecessors still live in Chapel Hill—Bill Aycock, Nelson Ferebee Taylor, Chris Fordham, and Paul Hardin III—along with Nancy Sitterson and Carmen Hooker, who remain such an integral part of the Carolina family. And all of us owe a special thanks to Interim Chancellor Bill McCoy, who brought stability and strong leadership in the wake of the tragic death of Chancellor Michael Hooker, and former Provost Dick Richardson, who demonstrated uncommon devotion to Carolina during his tenure, especially in those closing months.

Today's Defining Issue: The Bond Referendum

Today, we again have before us a defining moment. I speak, of course, of the 3.1-billion-dollar bond referendum for higher education that North Carolina's voters will consider on November 7th.

Indeed, this is a defining moment for all of higher education in North Carolina, for the future of this state. This is about maintaining our commitment to access and opportunity for all North Carolinians.

For Carolina, the referendum is about being able to accept our fair share of the expected enrollment surge over the next decade. It is about modernizing 120 classrooms and lecture halls, so that 21st-century students can learn in a 21st-century environment.

It is also about providing modern research space for our faculty who produce the new knowledge that will affect the lives of every North Carolinian, every American. I have visited the laboratories of faculty who are doing cutting-edge research that has the potential to cure diseases and improve all of our lives, work that is hampered by the physical limitations of old buildings not suited for today's science. The good news is that these faculty are just as loyal to Carolina as the faculty who stuck with us during the Great Depression. They have faith that the people of North Carolina will once again rise to the challenge and invest in the future.

Considering how much our faculty in chemistry and biological sciences, for example, have done with inadequate buildings, creating world-class teaching and research programs, one can only imagine what they can accomplish when freed from such limitations.

The bond bill is the key that opens the lock to the future. Almost half a billion dollars would come directly to this campus.[1] My pledge to the people of North Carolina is to take that investment and triple it in private support to this university through our upcoming campaign.

The bond referendum and our campaign set the stage for what can be a profound transformation of the university in the new century, a defining moment of major proportion.

The Vision of Preeminence

In his short time here, Chancellor Hooker revitalized the intellectual climate at Carolina. He strengthened this university's connection with every corner of the state. And—I think this was his greatest contribution—he dared us to think big. He articulated the vision of Carolina being the best public university in America. Some said it was an impossible reach or that it was too focused on journalistic ratings. Others questioned the qualifier "public." Why not try to be the best among all universities, they asked.

In my earliest conversations with the search committee it was the audacity of that vision that caught my attention. As the authors of one book on management have written, those institutions that become dominant in their field do so by adopting "big, hairy, audacious goals." This vision certainly fits the definition.

Chancellors can articulate visions, but it takes all of us—students, faculty, staff, and our alumni and friends—to make it happen. So allow me to use the balance of my time making the case for a new articulation of the vision.

The Pursuit of Excellence

First, let us agree that we will cling proudly to that word *public*. While we will compete with the private as well as public universities for students, faculty, and resources, we shall never depart from our roots as the university for the people.

Second, let us avoid bowing before the altars of the false gods of journalistic ratings. We must not allow ourselves to become preoccupied with comparisons to other universities. By so doing, we run the grave risk of losing what sets Chapel Hill apart and makes it so special.

To be sure, we cannot avoid altogether the attention paid to surveys, and we can hardly resist mentioning them when we rank near the top. Some of these exercises have scholarly credibility. For example, a recent University of Florida analysis laid out nine performance measures when examining public and private universities: total research expenditures, federal research expenditures, endowment assets, annual giving, number of faculty in the national academies, faculty awards, doctoral degrees, postdoctoral appointees, and freshman median SAT scores.

By those standards, Carolina was one of only four publics, along with Berkeley, UCLA, and Michigan, to place in the top 25 of all public campuses in each of the nine categories. But those are just nine measures. At Carolina, we should aspire to the highest levels of excellence in everything we do—in educating our students, advancing the frontiers of knowledge, and serving the public that supports us.

We Serve by Leading

Numbers alone fail to capture the essence of a great university—no matter how well intentioned the logic that led to their calculations in the first place. Other more profound characteristics are harder to pinpoint. Ultimately, it is these intangible criteria that should capture our attention.

What then makes a university stand out amongst all its peers? What makes it preeminent? How will we define this for Carolina?

We must lead. We must aspire for the highest levels of performance and service.

Carolina has always been a leader, beginning with the very creation of public higher education 207 years ago. We must continue to be out front in the critical new areas of discovery that will mark the new century. And we must constantly reconnect the process of discovery with engagement across the state and nation. Edward Kidder Graham articulated this clearly in 1915, and Chapel Hill led the South by its early example of engagement. Thus, we will set our course for the future by drawing deeply upon the wells of our own tradition.

Let me suggest that there are several distinctive and characteristic ways in which Chapel Hill has led and will continue to lead in the future.

A University with Core Values

First, this university has always had the courage of its convictions. It has embraced certain core values, even when those values were not fully understood by the popular culture. In 1925, President Chase was under fire for espousing the teaching of evolution. A young Frank Porter Graham rose to his defense, writing to local newspapers: "[Chase] has raised the university standard to be seen by all our people. Freedom to think, freedom to speak, and freedom to print are the texture of that standard. [...] It is the cornerstone and motto of the first American university to open its doors in the name of the people [...] *Lux Libertas* is cut with native chisel deep in the stones quarried from local soil."

Howard Odum's pioneering work in social science research challenged the values and mores of the old South, and in so doing, led the South out of its past and into a brighter future. In the 1950s, we again showed the South the way, opening our doors to students of all races and beginning a journey toward the creation of a diverse culture. Carolina students were among the first to fight against the Speaker Ban Law that threatened First Amendment rights in this state and threatened to kill free inquiry on campus.

This university will continue to lead in the 21st century—leading the discussion of the critical social and ethical issues that mark our time, defending freedom, and subjecting the dogmas and dictums of our time to the light of truth and reason. We shall also lead by including students in our discussion of values, so that their experience on this campus may lead to a profound and transforming development of their own character, remembering always that this is why we were created two centuries ago. The greatest names, to mention just three, in our academic pantheon—Odum, Venable, Horace Williams—are remembered not just as scholars, but as teachers.

Excellence and Engagement

Second, this university has developed a culture of unwavering commitment to excellence. We must constantly reaffirm that commitment. To meet this standard, every academic program we offer should be at the very highest level of excellence. A truly great university will have no identifiable areas of weakness. Any programs in our repertoire must be aimed at being consistently in the top tier as judged by the appropriate national peer groups, such as the National Research Council. That is a high standard, but an essential one for a university with such lofty aspirations. The corollary to this is equally clear. We must move resources to shore up any faltering programs to keep them at the top level.

We must maintain strength in all of the core areas in arts and sciences from which the university's great reputation initially sprang. Our pioneering work in the social sciences established Chapel Hill as a national colossus in these fields. Our strengths in the humanities are legendary, and our library holdings in several areas are without compare. We must continue to build on these strong foundations with the goal that Carolina's great history will guide the excellence we pursue in the future. For example, Chapel Hill has always been the place to come to study the American South. We must commit ourselves to the proposition that it always will be, even as our region determines its proper role in the global age.

Carolina's historical strengths in the basic and health sciences present great opportunity for leadership in such critical fields as genomics; nanotechnology; computational, environmental, and materials science; and emerging technologies. Our potential is limited only by inadequate physical spaces for science.

Francis Collins, the Carolina graduate who has so ably directed the nation's Human Genome Project, has called the efforts to sequence the human genome a milestone for biology like no other. Carolina must seize the initiative and emerge as a leader in genomics, and I am pleased to say that we are on the way. We already have successfully convinced some of the world's top minds that Chapel Hill's collaborative culture is worth the move. And we have just allocated 18 new faculty positions to our genomics initiative that will bring together the College of Arts and Sciences and the schools of medicine, dentistry, nursing, pharmacy, public health, and information and library science. That exciting development illustrates perfectly how fortunate we are to have an academic culture that fosters interdisciplinary work between and among the health, natural, and social sciences. Now more than ever before, we also need to draw upon the humanities as well, as these emerging fields raise new value-laden questions about the nature of life itself. Only a truly great university can bring all the resources needed to examine these issues from all perspectives. We intend to be that university.

We must also find ways to extend the reach of research beyond campus. Our technology transfer activities and alliances with private industry must become increasingly sophisticated. Names like Micell, Xanthon, and Inspire are a source of pride, because they represent success in spinning off our research to the national marketplace. In the process, we have used advancements in carbon dioxide and genomics technology, as well as drug development, to help create jobs, bolster North Carolina's economy, and bring products to consumers in new ways. Such success is a credit to our faculty's ability to touch the lives of people through discovery.

Leading requires collaboration and cooperation with other institutions.

We must continue to pursue active partnerships with our peers in the Research Triangle—Duke, NC State, and NC Central—and we should look boldly for opportunities to work with our sister UNC campuses as well as with North Carolina's excellent community college system.

A Vibrant Learning Community

Most critically, Carolina has been known historically as an institution that provided an unsurpassed student experience, earning the moniker "public ivy." We have taken the sons and daughters of mill workers and farmers and turned them into leaders for the state and nation.

The truly great university has an electricity about it, a force field of inquiry and discourse, that one literally feels when walking on its campus. It is a place where serious questions are being raised—where undergraduates are drawn into the process of discovery and engaged in a discourse that leads them in their individual paths of character development and citizenship. It is a place that nurtures and celebrates the arts.

I have already alluded to the faculty-led Task Force on Intellectual Climate. "The essence of a university is defined by its intellectual life," the task force's report began. While it was sobering in its assessment of that climate in 1997, it was visionary in its case for change. Most of its recommendations have been and are being implemented. First-year seminars are introducing our freshmen to the intellectual life of the university in small classes taught by the most distinguished faculty. We have established the Office of Undergraduate Research, the Academy of Distinguished Teaching Scholars, and the Carolina Center for Public Service. Later this fall, we shall break ground on new residence halls that will further integrate learning with living. We are still a work in progress in fulfilling the task force's suggestions, but we should all be pleased with the improvements so far and the serious commitment to the vision.

We are well under way in implementing the Carolina Computing Initiative—a first for a major public research university—as a means of transforming the learning environment for students and faculty. We are placing computers in the lap of every undergraduate and making tools available to arts and sciences faculty that will help them integrate technology into their classrooms. Now it is also time to put the world in their laps—to work toward the day when every Carolina undergraduate will have the opportunity to pursue a meaningful international experience. We must extend the international reach of this university if we are going to continue to lead. Consider the possibilities, for example, if every undergraduate had the opportunity to study abroad.

Chapel Hill helped lead the South into the 20th century. We must continue that legacy by creating, fostering, and sustaining a diverse community at Carolina. When I first met students in August, I urged them to talk with others from different ethnic or social backgrounds to broaden their own experiences, to come out of their individual comfort zones, and, in the process, build a more diverse and understanding community, one person at a time. This is only a critical first step. Our community here must reflect the real world, and we must provide opportunities for students of different cultures and backgrounds to live and work together in such a way that the campus becomes a true model for a multicultural, pluralistic society. America's most intractable problems still revolve around race and class. Our leadership—drawn from the wisdom of our past and the experiences we can all learn from today—is still sorely needed across the region and beyond.

The Carolina Spirit

As I have walked our brick paths and talked with faculty and staff in their laboratories and offices, with students in quads, residence halls, and the Pit, and with our alumni across the state, I have discovered something utterly unique about Carolina. As a newcomer, I may see it more clearly: not only is the sky bluer here than anywhere else in the world—(the fact that people really believe it to be so is part of what I am talking about)—but there is an atmosphere, a spirit on this campus that I have not seen or felt on any other campus in America.

I have seen it in the eyes of our alumni, our students, and our faculty. I have also seen it in our staff, who continue to amaze me with their devotion and dedication to Carolina.

I am almost afraid to describe this, lest by calling attention to it we might somehow damage or destroy it. Some might call it a spirit of optimism. It includes a special love of the place, a reverence for its history and tradition, not just of the physical but the spiritual place of a university that has truly been a light on the hill—a light for truth and social justice.

A New Defining Moment

We have a wonderful history, a noble tradition. I can feel it when I walk this campus in the still of the evening, and in the mid-day, when it is alive with students crossing Polk Place. I can feel it now, and I am in awe of it.

A university is a living organism that must be constantly re-created and regenerated. We are not building from scratch—as did Davie—or steering through crisis—as did Spencer and Graham. We are, rather, standing upon their shoulders as we enter a new century. We have before us the potential of a new defining moment for Carolina—the possibility of being not only the first, but the best, the leading, the preeminent public university in America.

It starts with the bonds, it continues with a massive outpouring of support from alumni and friends, and it finds fulfillment in our dedication, our aspiration to lead, to be the best—not in any sense of pridefulness or arrogance—but in the humility and dedication to service without any recompense, as in the words of Micah: to do justice and to love mercy.

In that spirit, I accept the challenge of leading this great university into a new age.

Lux. Libertas. Light. Liberty.

"Hail to the brightest star of all [...] Carolina, priceless gem."

Note

1. Actually, Carolina received slightly more than $525 million for construction and renovation from the North Carolina Higher Education Bond.

2001 STATE OF THE UNIVERSITY ADDRESS

The University of North Carolina at Chapel Hill
September 5, 2001

*F*OLLOWING THE INSTALLATION ADDRESS, *in my second year, I delivered the first "State of the University Address." The reader will note the change in political climate from the year before. As of this date of delivery, the General Assembly was still wrestling with the budget shortfalls, and it was clear that UNC's budget would be cut. Also, one will see several references to the retention of "overhead receipts,"—Federal reimbursements for the indirect costs of conducting research. Some in the General Assembly (and also in the UNC General Administration) viewed these reimbursements as a source for solving the state's budgetary shortfalls. This became a major struggle.*

The Campus Development Plan is mentioned in the address. Before Carolina could embark on its ambitious program of new construction, it had to get relief from the Town of Chapel Hill, which had a solid lid on any new campus development. Few major research universities have ever faced such a difficult political situation. The town had the power to block everything we wanted to do, so we engaged in very direct and delicate negotiations with the Town of Chapel Hill, represented by a team led by the Mayor, and the University, led by the Chancellor. At the outset, it was not at all clear that we would succeed. (There was always the subtle threat of a "nuclear option"—going to the General Assembly to strip the town of its power, but we were able to succeed diplomatically without going to war. I will always believe, however, that the specter of intervention by our powerful friends in Raleigh helped us to succeed.)

Toward the end of this address, I took advantage of my bully pulpit to speak out on some controversial social issues of the day—capital punishment and the inclusion of sexual orientation as part of UNC's non-discrimination policy, long before it was included. Not all presidents and chancellors agree that it is appropriate to speak out in such a setting on major social issues which can be controversial. For me, it was an invocation of the historic culture of Carolina, as embodied in our pantheon of heroes, notably Graham, Odom, and Friday.

What we could not have known, of course, is that on September 11, 2001, the world would change with the attacks on the World Trade Center. The planned University Day announcement of the major fundraising effort (what became known as the Carolina First Campaign) would be postponed for a full year because of 9/11.

THANK YOU FOR JOINING me today. As another school year begins and I have just marked my one-year anniversary in Chapel Hill, I cannot think of a better time to look at where Carolina has been and, perhaps more importantly, where it is going. Today's State of the University address does that.

I am indebted to Professor Estroff for a provocative article in the July–August *Carolina Alumni Review*. Sue noted Carolina's special culture that I think all of us celebrate: a culture of community and concern for human values. We participate in a covenant of generosity with the people of North Carolina, she wrote, "a generosity that is both personal and intellectual. We know how to work together, and we take a genuine pleasure in the accomplishments of the individuals who make up our community."[1]

At an institution I served previously, I tried to make the case that a culture of excellence was best typified by that very feature: the genuine pride in the accomplishments of others—one's colleagues or one's students. At the time, I did not realize that what I was describing was Carolina.

Indeed, last year I heard one of this university's most distinguished research faculty members say that this was our secret weapon, our strong tradition of working together across departmental and divisional lines and not caring who gets the credit.

Carolina also has a reputation as a place that values learning for its own sake, a place where the joy of learning is overtly evident in all we do—in the classroom, the laboratory, the residence hall, and all places in between. This is special and something we should cherish and celebrate. I have been a part of several other academic communities, and I have never known one that comes even close to what I can feel here—morale that is buoyant and optimistic, a genuine pride in association with one's colleagues and the university itself.

Last year a senior faculty colleague explained it to me this way. "Chancellor," he said, "do you have any idea what it feels like when I go to my national meeting and say, 'I am from Chapel Hill,' and people turn in respect and admiration?" Of course, it is the collective eminence of the faculty that created that reputation in the first place. A year later, I can honestly answer that question. "Yes, I do know how that feels. There is pride in saying, 'I'm from Chapel Hill.'" There is also great humility in standing before you as your chancellor.

That same pride can be felt among our students and the staff. I have seen it up close during events like the Chancellor's Student Award ceremony last spring and, just a few weeks ago, during my first opportunity to present Chancellor's Awards to five outstanding faculty and staff. This is a special place. There is a magic here. I love how Frank Porter Graham described it: "There is music in the air of the place,"[2] he said.

Yes, we do have a wonderful culture and tradition here at Carolina, what I would call a symphonic culture of excellence. This culture is fragile and must not be taken for granted. But what caught my attention in Sue Estroff's article was not her evocation of the good that we know, but the challenge we face to pursue change without fear, even though we know it must inevitably involve risks.

To that end, let me outline the key challenges and opportunities facing all of us in this academic year:

- We must assess our funding needs in the context of the current legislative session while simultaneously moving forward boldly into the most ambitious fundraising campaign in our history.
- We have launched a process to create an academic plan reflecting campus-wide priorities that is thoughtful, comprehensive, and includes the broad participation of the academic community.
- We must move forward with the full realization of our visionary development plan that will guide the controlled, responsible physical growth for the next decade.

There are many other challenges, but I believe these are the most pressing and require our collective attention as a community during this current academic year.

In the light of the legislative session, let me pose a fundamental question for us to consider: Where do we stand with the people of North Carolina? Our state's entire educational system has been under intense scrutiny as our legislators have wrestled with extremely difficult questions about the state's current and future financial picture. Last fall, citizens ratified the higher education bond referendum by a 3–1 vote, passing this landmark legislation in all 100 counties. Yet, at times during the legislative session, this University was literally placed on the chopping block, threatened by cuts—real and proposed—that could quickly eradicate the years of work that allowed Carolina to rise to the status of a great public university. We have serious work to do in taking the University's story—in particular, the story of why research universities are so important—to both the people and the policymakers of our state. Over the summer and in these past few days we have been fighting to make sure that this voice has been heard; every member of the team, the faculty and staff leadership, our student leaders, our trustees, and our alumni and friends across the state—have battled to make the case that a great people deserve a great university.

With respect to the state budget debate, a final resolution continues to elude us, even as I speak today. The state's revenue picture worsened considerably as the summer wore on, sparking a protracted debate in Raleigh over tax increases. In the end, the budget package likely to be approved will probably contain mixed news for us. Tuition for our undergraduates will increase 5 percent for residents and just over 8 percent for non-residents above the rates previously approved last academic year by our campus and by the Board of Governors. We will serve our constituents with fewer staff—almost 3 percent fewer. Although we appear to have preserved our overhead receipts—those reimbursements earned by our faculty for the cost of conducting outside research—our ability to keep such revenue will be challenged again and again. On the positive side, the university will receive funding increases to support enrollment growth. My conclusion about this session is simply that it raises more questions about our state's priorities than it answers. This is clearly a time for vision and courage in North Carolina.

This university has been tested before. In the depths of the Great Depression, Frank Porter Graham recognized that declining revenue was not a sufficient reason to raid our intellectual resources. Said Graham, "Restoration of the vigor of an institution is slow and costly. Because a child survived on two meals a day is not a sound reason to put the child on less food."[3] With vision, courage, and leadership, Carolina survived that test and went on to enter a great period of growth and development that led to the modern university we know today.

The Vision for Carolina

The challenge today is not to become distracted by these short-term issues from our long-term vision for Carolina. What is that vision? It is to do what Carolina has always done best: to lead. The first public university in America should today be first among America's public universities. That is our history; that is our destiny.

Let me be clear: this vision has nothing to do with journalistic rankings. The latest *U.S. News and World Report* magazine rankings become public tomorrow night and will be covered by the news media in the coming days. If you must, read what the magazine has to say about us, but let us not for a second be diverted by these arbitrary and artificial ratings from the substance of our vision for excellence.

When we achieve that vision—of leading the way for America's great public universities—those benefiting the most will be the people of North Carolina and the future generations of North Carolinians who come through Chapel Hill.

If knowledge is the capital of our new economy, research universities are the source of that capital and will be at the center of thriving economies. We know that. We understand that, but we must make sure that the people and their elected officials understand that too. It is our duty and responsibility to share such knowledge. The burden lies with us to explain effectively how what we do here improves the daily lives of the people of North Carolina and beyond.

As a public university, Carolina cannot operate in a vacuum. We must recognize the pressures that state government faces. Our plea to the state is for financial stability and freedom from micromanagement. Threats of 7 percent cuts, even if unrealized, depict great financial instability and send shock waves that are felt not only here at home, but around the world as we seek to recruit the best and brightest faculty, staff, and students. Attempts to divert our overhead receipts from grants to other state needs do great harm to the productivity of our faculty, who last year averaged bringing into the university $149,000 per capita in external, peer-reviewed competitive grants.

Stability from the state would give us a platform of funding adjusted for inflation and future enrollment growth. With that platform of stability, we would do the rest. Last year, I made a pledge to the people of North Carolina that we would triple the impact of the bond issue on this campus with private fundraising. We intend to keep that pledge. I would further pledge that if we can achieve the financial stability I am describing, Carolina will do the rest in finding additional funds that can make the critical margin of excellence.

Clearly, we must continue with graduated and measured campus-initiated increases in tuition over the next several years to address issues about the quality of the education we provide. We will remain faithful to the State Constitution by allocating a sufficient portion of that revenue to need-based financial aid so no student is denied access to Carolina because of financial need. Later this fall, we shall take to the Board of Trustees an updated five-year plan for tuition necessary to support excellence.

Just in this past year, we have lost significant ground with salaries and benefits. Over the next five years, approximately one-third of our faculty will reach retirement age, and we will be competing with the other great universities across the country for the next generation of faculty. We also seek the flexibility to make salaries and benefits for our dedicated staff competitive in this tough Triangle labor market. This year our staff will receive only a modest pay increase that will not even cover the cost of their rising health insurance premiums. Some employees tell me they are worried about the affordability of basic health insurance. That is unacceptable. We must keep fighting for competitive and equitable compensation packages.

On University Day, we will unveil the public phase of our major fundraising campaign, the largest in our history. On that day, we will announce the results of our efforts in the "quiet phase" of this campaign, as well as the overall goal which will, more than anything else, define Carolina's future. This campaign will put us at the very forefront of public universities seeking private support. It will make us more competitive in recruiting the best minds—students, faculty, and staff. We shall seek 200 new endowed professorships (a nearly 70 percent increase over our current complement) and 1,000 new scholarships and fellowships. Think of the impact! Those numbers help demonstrate how this campaign will help meet our academic goals. It will also help fund the research and public service that will enable Carolina to make our state and our world a better place. And indeed, this effort will determine whether or not we reach our ultimate vision.

All of you are invited to help us celebrate Carolina's 208th birthday on University Day, October 12th. This is a great day in the life of the university, and this year will mark the beginning of our future—what can be Carolina's Golden Age, if we are all successful. Please be there.

Research Growth

The research productivity of Carolina's faculty continues growing at a steady pace. Last year, our research funding increased 9 percent overall, spurred largely by an impressive 20 percent boost from the National Institutes of Health. Last year, peer-reviewed external funding reached $375 million, and all signs indicate that this year will show another healthy gain. Just yesterday, we announced a new $26 million federally funded study led by Etta Pisano in medicine. The goal is to save lives of women who develop breast cancer by determining the effectiveness of digital mammography. Such exciting work demonstrates the excellence of our faculty.

Much of the research funding growth in the last three years has resulted from the re-investment of our overhead receipts from federally funded grants to construct new research facilities in the basic and health sciences. These dollars are our seed corn, our investment for the future. That is why we have fought so hard (and will continue to fight) to prevent the diversion of those funds to other portions of the state budget.

Our research is making its way directly to the North Carolina economy at an accelerated pace through the creation of tax-paying, for-profit spin-off companies that are solving local, state, and national problems and creating new jobs. Last year alone, technology developed in Carolina research programs spawned a dozen new companies.

Success stories abound, carrying with them important economic development and educational messages. Consider Holden Thorp, an award-winning chemistry professor whose research led to the creation of Xanthon, Inc., which is commercializing a patented electrochemical detection technology to analyze DNA, RNA, and proteins. Now Thorp has turned his experiences in growing that business into the topic of a new first-year seminar.

Also in chemistry, research conducted by Joe DeSimone and two of his students led to Micell Technologies several years ago. Among many results of that research, perhaps the most impressive has been DuPont's expansion of its Bladen County site with a $40 million Teflon facility. Ultimately, plans call for a total investment of $275 million and 100 permanent jobs.

Other distinguished Carolina scientists have made discoveries with important implications for the marketplace and the public. Let me quickly mention just a few:

- Richard Boucher in medicine just spun off his second company, CyFi, Inc., a start-up pursuing technology he developed with applications in chronic bronchitis and other respiratory diseases.
- Khalid Ishaq in pharmacy was instrumental in helping Wake Forest colleagues launch Kucera Pharmaceutical Company, which is coupling new compounds with existing drugs to increase their effectiveness against cancer and viruses including HIV/AIDS.
- Timm Crowder, who only recently left the ranks of our graduate students and is now in biomedical engineering, just had dry powder inhaler technology he helped invent turn into Oriel, Inc., which is seeking funding for commercial applications.
- Otto Zhou in physics developed technology that resulted in Applied Nanotechnologies, Inc., which is devising industrial applications for carbon nanotubes that include electrodes for batteries and gas discharge tubes for telecommunications circuit protection.
- Also in the rapidly emerging area of nanotechnology, consider the success of our nanoManipulator user interface technology, marketed through 3rd Tech Inc., which won an R&D 100 Award for licensed technology and is based on the outstanding work of Richard Superfine, Russ Taylor, and Sean Washburn from physics and computer science.

Ultimately, we want to do even more to get Carolina-created technology into the hands of the public, and our goal is to create our own venture capital fund and incubator space to further stimulate this kind of activity.

Those examples just briefly touch on the many positive ways in which our faculty are helping bolster the North Carolina economy. We should aggressively pursue the transfer of our technology—through licensing agreements, patent activity, and the like—into the marketplace to get those products into the hands of consumers who need them while at the same time generating revenue for the university to continue conducting research.

But there are limits, ethical and moral limits, raised by research and its ownership. What are the proper boundaries of patent rights and royalties? Who should benefit from discoveries involving the human body?[4] Those are questions a great university like Carolina should address.

Academic Planning

A key activity that should engage us all will be the development of the academic plan. This far-reaching effort will distill our current areas of strength and use our best thinking to pinpoint future areas of opportunity where Carolina can shine.

Provost Robert Shelton will lead this work. This plan should represent our vision—not my vision, not the Provost's, but our collective vision—resulting from the collaboration and engagement of the entire academic community. I hope you will consider this my invitation to join in this important process.

This is also an opportunity to restate my commitment to the tradition of shared governance at Carolina. We have a wonderful culture of collegiality, where faculty, staff, and students have an opportunity to participate meaningfully in decisions that broadly affect the campus. Let us all commit ourselves to the preservation of that culture.

Development Plan

Questions about our physical growth provide just such an example. Development of our master plan involved community participation and input—both on and off campus—for more than three years. That paid big dividends because the final plan benefited enormously from such an open and participatory process. The same will be true about the Horace Williams tract planning process, which will now be led by Vice Chancellor for Research and Graduate Studies Tony Waldrop.

On October 3rd, the Chapel Hill Town Council will vote on our development plan, which we have submitted in accordance with the ordinance approved in July to rezone the central campus. If approved, the plan will allow us to move forward over the next decade to realize the physical building of the campus, including critical bond-funded projects, essential new research buildings, major new cultural facilities for the benefit of the larger community, undergraduate residence halls, student family housing, and parking facilities. Ultimately, we aim to create a campus that is even more beautiful than the one we love today with a South Campus that is more welcoming to the students and families who live there as well as to the patients traveling here from afar.

As you know, our neighbors in Chapel Hill, many of whom are also members of our own faculty and staff, have great interest in this plan, especially where it abuts individual neighborhoods. The university has adjusted the plan in recognition of many neighbors' concerns. In the Mason Farm neighborhood, we are committed to working with residents in discussing design plans for the student family housing along Mason Farm Road. We believe that graduate students and their families will be excellent neighbors. All of us have concerns about growth. All of us understand the tension between the desire to keep things the way they are and the need for progress and improvement. We look forward to working with the neighbors on all sides of campus.

Let me take this opportunity to bring you up to date. Our staff has been deeply engaged in follow-up work since the July zoning vote to submit the development plan and a lengthy addendum that provided additional data, maps, and other information responding to questions that arose based on the town's review and neighborhood concerns. We have learned recently of additional stipulations that go beyond mutually agreed upon guidelines and standards that described the university's responsibilities for mitigating the impact of growth. These stipulations appear to shift costs disproportionately to the university, its students, and ultimately the state.

I am concerned about these reports and a process that conditions approval of our development plan with requirements beyond the standards that were negotiated in good faith during the rezoning of our campus. I remain hopeful that we can continue to work productively. For now, I would be remiss if I did not thank the dozens of university employees in multiple units who have toiled long and hard on many nights and weekends this summer to make possible our submission of the development plan and the nearly equally long addendum. They have also handled our responses to questions and requests from the town and community with aplomb. In particular, I wish to single out the exemplary work of Vice Chancellor Suttenfield, Associate Vice Chancellors Bruce Runberg and Carolyn Elfland, and their colleagues.

The information I have just shared demonstrates why it is so important for all of you to learn more about our development plan. I urge you to attend a campus-wide forum on September 10th at 5:30 p.m. in the Carroll Hall auditorium. The forum is sponsored by the Faculty Council, Employee Forum, and Student Government. It is important for the university community to be well-informed about this issue and its implications on campus as well as in the community that we love and live in together.

The Arts and Humanities

We have focused a great deal on the sciences over the past year—our $245 million investment in genomics, our great strengths in nanotechnology, computer sciences, and the environmental sciences, among others—but I fear that we have left unsaid our equal commitment to the arts and humanities at Carolina. Lest there be any doubt, let me be quite specific: I do not believe that we can be America's best public university on the strength of science alone. Indeed, without an equal commitment to excellence in the arts and humanities, one might—with good reason—question where our values lie. Lest we fall into the trap of putting everything into quantitative terms, let us ask the question, what is the value to our society of the unfunded, but nonetheless significant research of our artists and humanists? What is the value of a sonnet, or a sonata?

This university has not nurtured the arts as it should. That has become clear to me over the past year. With the exception of the PlayMakers Repertory Company, which has few—if any—peers among American universities, our programs in the arts have been neglected, especially from a standpoint of their physical facilities. The bond issue will ultimately rectify the deplorable state of the music library, which houses one of the most distinguished collections in America, but it does nothing for the Department of Music's performance facilities, which remain sub-par. Likewise, the Ackland Art Museum, which has enormous potential for education in the visual arts, is in dire need of renovation and expansion. These projects will be addressed through the fund-raising campaign.

If the arts are the heart of the university, the humanities are the very soul of Carolina. Carolina's strengths in these areas are legendary. We must also pay careful attention to our library, whose holdings are without compare in many areas. Never again should we put the library at risk when budget cuts threaten, no matter how severe the situation. The library must be and continue to be one of our major priorities. We cannot be a great university without a great library.

We must also be a world university. The great universities of the world will be judged on an international stage. That means we must offer a truly superior international education at Chapel Hill, an education that will remain rooted in the finest Carolina tradition, but that will prepare our state and our students for leading in a global economy. Carolina is making immense progress in becoming a great international university, with major new joint programs involving the College of Arts and Sciences and the schools of public health; journalism and mass communication; education; information and library science; and business with the Monterrey Institute of Technology System, Mexico's top technology university, as just one example. Another example of our growing international stature is evident through a proposal now being shepherded by the Kenan-Flagler Business School and the College of Arts and Sciences to establish an undergraduate business degree program in Qatar. The project resulted from an invitation by the Qatar Foundation, which would pay all expenses associated with the venture. Provost Shelton has appointed a committee comprised of representatives from the Kenan-Flagler Business School and the College of Arts and Sciences to develop an appropriate curriculum to support such a program. This represents the kind of international opportunities that can serve as a model for the university abroad and help establish our global presence in a meaningful way.

Engagement

I also see a renewed interest in public service on campus. This past year, a group of students from the APPLES service-learning program came to see me to tell me what they were doing and to urge me to do all that I could to make sure faculty who integrate service into learning are properly recognized and rewarded for it. There is a growing recognition that active service enhances the learning environment.

I am proud of the commitment to service I see at Carolina, a commitment that is unlike anything I have ever seen before. It is part of our tradition, first articulated by President Edward Kidder Graham, who simply said to the people of North Carolina: "Write to the university when you need help."[5] We must refocus on Carolina's service role, on our responsibility to engage the public, to solve the problems, and to make this world a better place.

I recently heard Gene Nichol, the dean of the Law School, make a telling observation in comparing Carolina to our other major national peers—the other great public universities. (You know them now by heart—Berkeley, UCLA, Michigan, and Virginia.) What sets us apart from each of these, Dean Nichol said, is that Carolina is the only one of this group that wants to be a public university. We embrace the word *public*.

We cannot—and at Carolina, I would argue, do not—consider engagement an option. It is an integral part of a great university's life, not something to be practiced when convenient or if the mood strikes us. We must remember Carolina's tradition of public service, and we must consider such service an obligation and responsibility, a debt we owe to the people of North Carolina as well as to society at large.

The Courage of Our Convictions

Finally, let me close with some thoughts about Carolina's noble legacy of moral leadership and how that legacy should help define our future. Chapel Hill helped define the new South, and in so doing defined itself, by having the moral courage to support controversial research that challenged mores and traditional values. We must be a university that holds contemporary culture up to the critical light in the context of freedom. Light and Liberty. Lux, Libertas.

In that light, we have a moral responsibility to our state and our nation as a public university to bring to the public square the great issues of our day, without fear of censorship. Just as Chancellor Aycock and President Friday worked to defeat the repression of free speech embodied in the Speaker Ban Law, and just as President Graham spoke out vehemently against the use of the atomic bomb, we must be willing to take a stand on critical issues of the day. We must be tolerant of the opinions expressed by others and ever supportive of their right to express them, but at the end of the day, we must have the courage and the fortitude to stand by our beliefs and act upon them.

Consider Carolina's role in leading the South out of its culture of racism, segregation, and Jim Crow. That work remains unfinished, for we still live with the lingering toxins of racism. Even today there are those who consider us a racist institution because of our own past. We can counter this only with a renewal of our strong commitment to freedom, to equality, equity, and to a society of pluralism. I am proud that 50 years ago this fall, Carolina became one of the first major Southern universities to open its doors to African-American students. Today, I am proud that Carolina is given the highest approval marks of any major public university by African-American students as reported by *Black Enterprise* magazine.[6] I am proud, too, that the Sonja Haynes Stone Black Cultural Center building is at last becoming a physical reality on campus, long since it has become a cultural and academic reality. Diversity is a vital component of our vision to become first among America's public universities, and we must all recommit ourselves to this important challenge every day.

I think the same moral responsibility points us directly to the great issues before us today. We should lead in asking these questions: How long will America be the last great nation of the developed world to practice capital punishment? Why should we hide our commitment to nondiscrimination based on a person's sexual orientation? Is it not time that we reclaimed the words "character" and "values" from the extreme right and put them back into the mainstream of secular, public higher education? These are among the questions of our time.

Yet it is not enough just to ask the questions. We must act on our convictions. This is the complex role of a truly great university: to be both a conservator of culture and values, and a leader of change, both in ourselves and in the larger society.

In so doing, we are faithful to our own traditions of excellence, engagement, and leadership. And thus, the university that became the model for public higher education in America will again be leading the way, to be the "light on the hill" for America and the world.

This is the vision of a great university, a university destined to lead—a university that embraces excellence in the creation and dissemination of knowledge, engaged with the people whom it serves, and grounded in human values and free expression. Together, let us embrace the vision. Let us be that university.

Notes

1. Estroff, Sue E. "The Long View." *Carolina Alumni Review*, July/August 2001, Vol. 90, No. 4, p. 42.
2. Graham, Frank Porter. "The University Today." Inaugural address delivered November 11, 1931. Printed in *The Alumni Review*, December, 1931, XX, No. 3, p. 110.
3. Ashby, Warren. *Frank Porter Graham: A Southern Liberal*. Winston-Salem, N.C.: John F. Blair, Publisher, 1980, p. 90.
4. Markel, Howard. "Patents Could Block the Way to a Cure." *New York Times*, August 24, 2001, national edition, A21.
5. Coates, Albert. *Edward Kidder Graham, Harry Woodburn Chase and Frank Porter Graham: Three Men in the Transition of the University of North Carolina at Chapel Hill from a Small College to a Great University*. Chapel Hill, N.C.: A. Coates, 1988, p. 12.
6. Whigham-Desir, Marjorie and Thomas A. LaVeist. "Making the Most of the Freshman Year." *Black Enterprise*, January 2001, Vol. 31, No. 6, pp. 64–75.

A TEMPEST IN A TEXTBOOK:
ACADEMIC FREEDOM AND THE QUR'AN CONTROVERSY

Remarks to the National Press Club, Washington, D.C.
August 27, 2002

*O*N *AUGUST 27, I was invited to speak before the National Press Club in Washington, remarks that were carried live by* C-SPAN *and the* BBC. *This was the culmination of months of controversy over the choice of a book,* Approaching the Qur'an, *by Michael Sells as the reading assignment for incoming first year students.* Fox News *broke the story about this assignment in May of 2002, and it quickly went viral. For me, this entire controversy was a teachable moment about the real purpose of public higher education in America, harkening back to our founding in 1789, coinciding with the signing of the U.S. Constitution. It was about First Amendment freedom and academic freedom.*

> Email to James_Moeser@unc.edu: "[...] Americans are not interested in foreign religions. Foreigners are, of course. Thanks for identifying UNC as an Islamic University."
> Email: "Not everyone's views are worth hearing. Muslims prove every day that Islam is a religion of violence and terror [...]"
> Email: "Islam needs [to be] destroyed, not taught."
> Email: "[...] After reading this article from the *Washington Post*, I took you off the list of colleges I am considering. [...] May you find a packet of anthrax and a pipe bomb in your mailbox. Thank you."
> Email: "I would like to know who the atheist idiot is that suggested

the teaching of the Koran in some college there in your state. [...] You might as well teach the full course of anti-Americanism."

Email: "Congratulations on choosing to become the 'Berkeley' of the East Coast. [...] I hope your enrollment plummets in the face of this idiotic decision."

Email: "I've thought for a long time that Islam could not exist in harmony with anyone. [...] but I was wrong. It'll fit just fine in the People's Republic of Chapel Hill."

And my all-time favorite:

Email: "You are doing the work of Satan, and you will surely perish in the lake of fire."

All of this because we asked our students to read a book. Some of you know this story, but for those who do not, let me quickly lay out the sequence of events in this controversy.

For the past four years, as part of an effort to enrich the intellectual climate at Chapel Hill, we have asked all new freshmen and transfer students to take part in a summer reading program. They read an assigned book before they come to campus. Then, the day before classes begin, they attend small discussion sessions about the book. Our goal is to create an early expectation among students that they will think critically and discuss different points of view throughout their time at UNC.

This year, we evidently did the unthinkable. We selected *Approaching the Qur'an: The Early Revelations*, by Michael Sells, a professor of religion at Haverford College. The reading assignment prompted a federal lawsuit from the Family Policy Network, a Christian group that claimed that UNC was advocating Islam, and thus violating the establishment clause of the Constitution. The House of Representatives of the North Carolina General Assembly attached a proviso to the budget to disallow the use of state funds for any program or course that deals with a single religion unless all known religions are given equal treatment. This proviso would affect many offerings in the Department of Religious Studies, which is one of the oldest and largest religion departments in any American public university. And in response to this clear threat to academic freedom, the Board of Governors of the 16-campus University of North Carolina system failed in an initial vote to endorse a resolution in support of academic freedom. (Last week, the Board of Governors' Committee on Education Planning, Policies and Programs unanimously approved a new motion reaffirming academic freedom.) Throughout it all, the letters, emails, and phone calls have poured in from across the country. Many, I am pleased to tell you, were supportive. But many had the flavor of those I read you earlier.

Then, on August 19, after the Family Policy Network's legal efforts to shut us down had failed, we went on with our discussion groups. We trusted our students' desire to read, to think and to learn.—And nothing terrible happened. If the intent of the program had been to convert students to Islam, it was a tragic failure. There were no known conversions. Carolina's religion remains basketball.

Did we know when we selected *Approaching the Qur'an* that it would be controversial? Yes. Did we know it would literally fuel a new round of national debate about academic freedom? Not in our wildest imaginations. But I am glad it did.

It is precisely in times like these in our history that it is important to reaffirm a university's role in addressing controversial subjects. One of the many newspaper headlines said it best: The University's Summer Reading Program is about ideas, not indoctrination. The role of the university is to educate, not to advocate. But an idea—especially an idea about religion, or an even more combustible mixture, religion and politics—is dangerous only when we don't have the critical thinking to examine it. We have a responsibility to students to provide an atmosphere in which they can deepen their sense of themselves and the complex, often contradictory, world around them. That's what the Summer Reading Program is designed to do. We want to create an intellectual climate in which students themselves can come to their own conclusions and turn information into insight.

So what happened in those discussion sessions?

Well, I can tell you about the discussion group I led. For two hours, twenty-five first-year students spoke respectfully and articulately about a wide range of perspectives, value systems, and beliefs. Students from Christian backgrounds compared notes with a Jewish student about a passage from *Approaching the Qur'an*. That discussion was prompted in part by comparison of a passage from the Qur'an, one of the suras, with a psalm from the Bible. We agreed on the similarity of themes in both texts such as one omniscient God, the ephemeral nature of life and the concept of redemption. The students also found interesting differences. One student recounted criticisms of the summer reading assignment by her friends and family. She participated anyway, she said, because she wanted to be educated. For many of our students, the biggest question of the day seemed to be: "What was all the fuss about?"

I felt enormous pride in our students for their diligence in preparation for a non-credit reading assignment and discussion—and for their unflappability in the face of national attention. I thought to myself: "These kids will be fine. This is a new generation of leaders." They are an enormous asset to North Carolina and to the other states they call home.

The University of North Carolina has long been credited with taking the sons and daughters of mill hands and farmers and preparing them to be leaders. This is our proud legacy. Ferrel Guillory, who heads UNC's Program on Southern Politics, Media and Public Life, in a piece in last Sunday's *Raleigh News and Observer*, points to John Egerton's book, *Speak Now Against the Day*, which is an account of the South in the 1930s, 40s, and 50s. Edgerton says in his book, "The single most glowing exception to broad-based mediocrity in the Southern academic world was the University of North Carolina at Chapel Hill. The University acquired a level of independence and quality that kept it in the front rank of public and private schools in the region."

It would be easy to misread the recent events in North Carolina and conclude that this is just another example of some backward Southern state, demonstrating its lack of tolerance for dissent or for progressive (and unpopular) ideas. Such a conclusion would badly miss the mark. To be sure, North Carolina, as Guillory points out in his *News & Observer* piece, has long been a state of internal conflicts and contradictions—a state that could simultaneously elect Jim Hunt and Jesse Helms. It is at the same time a conservative state and a modern progressive state. Some of America's leading financial institutions are based in North Carolina, and our medical centers are among the nation's best. Joining UNC-Chapel Hill is a great array of distinguished institutions of higher education in North Carolina—including Duke and NC State in the Triangle, Wake Forest, Davidson and several other universities in the UNC system.

Today, at Chapel Hill we still have students from very small towns, but we also have students from very sophisticated big-city schools in North Carolina, from the District of Columbia, from the other 49 states and 100 countries. But wherever they hail from, our students all come to Chapel Hill to learn about themselves and the world in an atmosphere of open, free and rigorous inquiry.

That atmosphere has served our students and the state of North Carolina exceedingly well. A leading public university fearlessly tackles subjects that make all of us a little uncomfortable. The only way we'll find answers to the really big issues facing our state, our nation, and our world is to create an environment of unfettered inquiry in which students learn to think critically, ask tough questions, and come to their own conclusions.

That's what we want. We want our students to taste the excitement of encountering new ideas. This year in the Summer Reading Program, we succeeded beyond our wildest dreams. Along the way, other important issues, including academic freedom, became a significant part of the story. And our students got to think about it and talk about it.

In short, we believed in our students. And they showed us that they have tremendous intellectual capacity. We put our trust completely in their desire to read, to think, and to learn. Suppressing that trust in any way would diminish the educational experience of all students, and it would diminish our nation's ability to respond to the many challenges it will face in the future. Ensuring that trust—and providing an environment in which difficult, relevant subjects may be discussed freely—is the university's very reason for existence.

Despite the success of the program, I am acutely aware that many people did not support the book selected for our summer reading assignment or what we were trying to accomplish in the discussions. Reasonable people can disagree about the choice of the book, and they do—both on campus and off campus. But we did not, and would not ever, take a public opinion poll before assigning a book if we felt that a particular book was important to the discussion of a particular topic.

The criticism leveled against the Sells book is that it is an incomplete picture of Islam, that it presents only the early suras, not the later ones, which are often used as a pretext for violence and terrorism. There is some merit to this charge. Remember that the purpose of this program was not to present the complete picture of the faith of Islam in a single reading and a two-hour discussion. That would be impossible.

Indeed, the reading itself and the discussions that have ensued raised many questions about Islam and Islamic fundamentalism. Where is the moderate Islamic voice? Is it being suppressed by the tide of Wahhabism that is dominant in some of the countries of the Middle East? These are good questions, and it is my hope that many of our students will be intrigued enough to pursue them with further study. That, after all, is the real purpose of the Summer Reading Program—to whet the appetite for learning and discovery.

The level of national controversy and media attention to this event could easily lead us to the false conclusion that we accomplished more than we did. This was only one book and one two-hour discussion, not for credit. In leading our students to a better understanding of the world, I think we may have moved one grain of sand. One grain of sand. But it was a start.

Now we hear that the Family Policy Network is at it again. Last week, the group attacked a reading assignment for new students at the University of Maryland, charging that in assigning *The Laramie Project* for Maryland students, the university is advocating a homosexual agenda. I wrote a note of support to President Dan Mote to extend my sympathy.

At least the FPN has good taste in universities. Throughout this controversy, a few of our critics have lumped UNC-Chapel Hill with the likes of Harvard and Berkeley. That's the kind of guilt by association that I can embrace.

Thank you for the opportunity to tell our story here today. I will be happy to answer questions.

2002 STATE OF THE UNIVERSITY ADDRESS

The University of North Carolina at Chapel Hill
September 4, 2002

*T*HIS ADDRESS WAS DELIVERED *only a week after my remarks to the National Press Club. The entire country was still consumed with the fear of terrorism, and at UNC there was remaining anxiety and controversy about the first-year reading assignment. In addition, we faced additional worry about looming budget cuts. The General Assembly was still in session trying to resolve the state's budget, even though Fiscal Year 2003 began on July 1, 2002. These two major concerns complicated my task in crafting this address. I had first to speak to those issues before I could begin to spell out more precisely the vision of being America's leading public university.*

For me, the controversy over the choice of a book was an opportunity to articulate Carolina's core values, harkening back to our creation in the 18th century. I drew upon my own remarks at my installation and in my 2001 State of the University address, and I cited the courageous stands taken by Presidents Frank Porter Graham and William Friday as well as Chancellor William Aycock, as precedent. I was delighted that both President Friday and Chancellor Aycock were present and that I could recognize them.

The fear of budget cuts was palpable. We had already seen massive cuts the previous year with the elimination of staff positions and a freeze on all expenditures imposed in May. At the same time, capital funds from the higher education construction bond continued to flow, adding to the confusion and low morale on campus. I needed to express sincere empathy with the faculty and staff who were most affected by these cuts.

About a third of the way into this address, I pivoted to a discussion of long-term goals and vision for the future, saying that we "cannot be so totally absorbed in our immediate problems that we lose sight of our long-term vision." Here, I contrasted management with leadership, and that took me to a discussion of what it means to be America's leading public university.

Even though the public announcement of the Carolina First Campaign was postponed to later in the fall of 2002, I was able to report some major success in this address from the silent phase of the campaign. I signaled a continuing commitment to public engagement—embracing our status as a public university as some of our peers were moving away from that acknowledgement.

I announced new Measures of Excellence, drafted in a retreat of deans and vice chancellors, and later approved by the Board of Trustees. These measures became the critical yardstick for progress toward our goals.

I spoke about the critical importance of raising faculty salaries and stemming the tide of great faculty being recruited away by other institutions. This became our major goal with the General Assembly and with the Carolina First Campaign.

External funding for research was already showing sharp increases. There was much to celebrate, and I used this address to launch a significant new investment in advanced materials, nanoscience and technology. I was also careful to say that our investments should not just be in big science, but also in the humanities, the social sciences, and the professions.

I ended this address with a return to the concept of a university with a moral compass, a university with a sense of public virtue. For me, it was a pastoral moment to speak to a community, troubled by circumstances of the times, about an inspiring vision for its future.

IT'S BEEN AN INCREDIBLE summer in Chapel Hill. It was just a year ago, September 5, when we gathered in this same space for my first State of the University Address. The biggest cloud on our horizon was the gaping hole in the state's budget. I addressed that issue early in the speech, and then moved on to raise the question of the long-term vision for Carolina, that of being the leading public university in America. I laid the groundwork for a major announcement on University Day of the goal for the Carolina First Campaign, and I concluded with thoughts about Carolina's noble legacy of moral leadership and how that legacy should help define our future.

Six days later, a catastrophic act of terrorism changed our world, altering the context of everything around us. To be sure, we still have a state budget crisis, and I shall address that again today, although rather briefly, since there are currently more questions than answers about the state of the state. We still have a great vision for Carolina, and I shall center my remarks on that, with the hope that this will begin a yearlong conversation among all of us about what precisely it will mean to be America's leading public university.

The major portion of this address will attempt to put some real flesh on the bones of this vision, some concrete measures that we can use to mark our progress. But, as I said last year, there are also some intangible and immeasurable aspects of a great university, elements of culture and climate. I shall conclude today with an invocation of ideals that lie at the heart of our culture and tradition—the idea that we exist for a higher purpose, as a bulwark of light and liberty undergirding freedom itself and serving, not ourselves, but the people of North Carolina and the United States. From this idea, we became "the university of the people."

Most fundamentally, this means having core values that shape our decisions and our actions, values that we are committed to defend and preserve. I concluded my remarks last year with a discussion of these characteristics, so let me begin today where I ended last year.

I said that Chapel Hill helped define the new South, and in so doing defined itself, by having the moral courage to support research that challenged the traditional mores and values of the South. "We must be," I said, "a university that holds contemporary culture up to the critical light in the context of freedom. Light and Liberty. *Lux, Libertas*."[1]

"In that light," I continued, "we have a moral responsibility to our state and our nation as a public university to bring to the public square the great issues of our day, without fear of censorship. Just as Chancellor Aycock and President Friday worked to defeat the repression of free speech embodied in the Speaker Ban Law, and just as President Graham spoke out vehemently against the use of the atomic bomb, we must be willing to take a stand on critical issues of the day. We must be tolerant of the opinions expressed by others and ever supportive of their right to express them. But at the end of the day, we must have the courage and the fortitude to stand by our beliefs and act upon them. [...]"

I am so pleased that we are joined today by two of these giants of our history, President Emeritus William Friday and former Chancellor Bill Aycock, two heroes for academic freedom at UNC.

I am also pleased and honored to recognize other former chancellors who could be with us today, upon whose shoulders we all stand. Let me ask Chris Fordham, Paul Hardin and Bill McCoy to stand.

The events of the past 12 months have made me proud to be your chancellor. I am proud of Carolina's response to the tragedy of September 11—the outpouring of more than 10,000 people in respectful silence in Polk Place; the demonstrations of patriotism and public service that sprang up all over campus; the individual and random acts of kindness, especially those directed toward members of our community who are Arab or Muslim; the seminars and teach-ins that asked probing questions about America and the world.

I am proud of Carolina for the courage to choose a book for the purpose of helping our students understand the complex and often contradictory forces that shape our world. Reasonable people can, of course, disagree about the choice of this book, but our intent was unmistakable from the beginning. We should extend our understanding to those who disagree with us. As William Sloane Coffin writes in a new book, "All of us tend to hold certainty dearer than truth. We want to learn only what we already know; we want to become only what we already are."[2]

On August 19th, our first-year and transfer students experienced what the Summer Reading Program intended—the excitement of discussing ideas. I was enormously proud of our students. They came prepared, they wrote excellent short essays, and they acquitted themselves well in vigorous discussion. Because of the national controversy that surrounded this event, it is easy to attach too much significance to it. In the global scheme of things, in the readings and the discussions, we may have moved one grain of sand toward our students' understanding of the world. But for many of them, it was a beginning.

Finally, I have been proud to speak for the entire community in defending our fundamental rights as Americans from any who would seek to limit the scope of free expression and inquiry. In the past 12 months, UNC has shown the world what it is to be a great, free, American public university. Last year, I had no idea when I said we should be a university with the courage of our convictions, that we would be tested within the year.

Throughout the controversy over the Summer Reading Program, most disheartening to us has been the charge that we were insensitive to the victims and families of September 11. Nothing could have been further from our intentions. Next week, on September 11, I invite you to come again to Polk Place at noon for a brief ceremony of reflection, remembrance and rededication to the principles of liberty and freedom; human dignity and equality; justice and peace. We shall honor the memory of the six Carolina alumni who perished in the World Trade Center and at the Pentagon, tolling the South Building bell once for each of them. Before and after the ceremony, a volunteer fair will take place in Polk Place with 75 diverse community and campus service organizations available to sign up new volunteers. I hope you will be there.

The State Budget

We have all watched with grave concern as the governor and members of the General Assembly have struggled with what many agree is the most critical financial environment for our state government since the Great Depression. North Carolina has experienced what some have called "the perfect storm" of bad economic news—a national recession, the decline of traditional state industries, several court decisions with major financial impact, and two major hurricanes, combined with massive tax cuts enacted in the 1990s and other fiscal challenges.

In fiscal year 2002, the state's budget woes directly resulted in more than $44 million worth of reductions on our campus. Nearly $10 million of that total constituted recurring reductions. The rest was from non-recurring funds or reversions from our state accounts, necessary because of the freeze placed on expenditures last May. Those losses meant we had to eliminate positions and people, delay other hiring, defer maintenance, reduce teaching, and cut programs.

I want to say something now about the great staff at this university whose work and loyalty contributes so much to the quality of the campus culture. You are the unsung heroes of a great university. You are the people who do everything from answering the telephones to maintaining the buildings and grounds to keeping our high-performance computer networks running efficiently. We are incredibly blessed with a wonderfully dedicated and underpaid staff.

Today, like the rest of the UNC system and state government, we are waiting to see what happens in Raleigh with the current deliberations about a resolution for a new budget for this fiscal year. We simply don't know what our exact budget cut will be yet, but we aim to protect core educational priorities. We hope to be left with the flexibility to decide for ourselves how to make additional cuts. And we hope the final measure preserves our overhead receipts, which are so vital to our research enterprise, to future growth at Carolina and, indeed, to the state's economy. We also remain deeply concerned about the impact of no salary increases and rising health-care insurance costs on our employees and their families.

Enrollment growth in the UNC system has been funded, at least in part, by increases in tuition, by action of the Board of Governors, which increased resident tuition 8 percent and non-resident tuition 12 percent. The leaders of both the Senate and the House have stated that tuition should not be used to fund enrollment growth, and they have committed themselves to including university enrollment growth as a part of the continuation budget in future years. We strongly support this move with the hope that tuition will not be used in the future as a means of funding enrollment growth in the system.

These are troubling times, but we cannot lose sight of Carolina's long-term prospects. Our state funding may be suffering, but we must continually remind ourselves that the people of North Carolina are investing a half-billion dollars in bond funds for new construction and renovations on this campus, guided by a visionary master plan. At the same time, our faculty continues to bring in record amounts of research dollars, and our alumni and friends are making wonderfully generous gifts to the university. We will weather this economic downturn.

We are preparing to launch a five-year financial plan. The goal is to align the resources we have in optimal fashion in order to accomplish the key academic goals of the university. In August, a new Tuition Advisory Task Force, composed of students, faculty, staff, and trustees, also began its work. This important panel is contemplating how campus-based tuition dollars can most appropriately be allocated to sustain and advance the university's ability to compete for the best faculty and students. The task force's charge is to consider a multi-year approach for such campus-based tuition increases, while balancing those competitive challenges with our historic commitment to keeping Chapel Hill's doors open to the sons and daughters of North Carolinians.

The Vision for UNC:
To Be America's Leading Public University

We have a responsibility to manage this university through these difficult times. We accept that responsibility. I believe that everyone at UNC, at every level of shared governance, is committed to managing our affairs through the current budgetary situation.

However, we also have a larger, more profound responsibility to keep our eyes on the more distant horizon, with a vision for the future. Indeed, our biggest challenge today is not to become so totally absorbed in our immediate problems that we lose sight of our long-term vision. This requires a kind of bifocal view of reality—a commitment to both responsible management and visionary leadership. Our vision is simple but profound—to be the leading public university in America.

Our Board of Trustees has embraced this vision. The steering committee of the Carolina First Campaign has been so inspired and uplifted by this vision that they have helped us generate over $846 million in new commitments to Carolina—89 newly endowed faculty chairs toward our goal of 200, more than 160 undergraduate scholarship funds and nearly 90 graduate fellowship funds. This October 11, a year later than originally planned, we shall finally make the public announcement of the campaign's goals. It is amazing to me, that in one of our economy's darkest periods, we have seen this incredible outpouring of support for Carolina.

The Board of Trustees and our committed volunteers are asking us some key questions: Are we raising the right money?—A question I interpret to mean, "Has the university clearly established its own priorities?" Related to this question is an even more probing one: What does it mean to be America's leading public university? How will we know when we have achieved our goal? Give us some measurable and quantifiable benchmarks that we can use to show our progress.

If Not *U.S. News and World Report*, Then What?

This is the conversation that I hope to begin today. We have already begun this discussion with the vice chancellors, cabinet, and deans in a retreat last month, and my desire today is to provoke an ongoing dialogue among faculty and staff, students and their parents, as well as our alumni and everyone who cares about this university.

The key word in this vision is *leading*—which carries multiple meanings. Leading implies an action, a sense of motion, rather than the goal of an end point. It signals leadership. This past year when we were the first major American university to call a halt to binding early decision admissions, we demonstrated leadership—moral leadership. We did it because it was the right thing to do: right for prospective students, right for their parents, right for America. I believe that others will follow, but whether or not they do, we have staked out the high ground on this issue. More recently, we chose a book because we believed it to be the right book for the right question. We started a national conversation about American values in the age of terrorism. We are leading.

The second key word in this vision is *public*. Some have argued that we should remove it from the description, and some of the public universities created in our image have, indeed, all but removed public from their self-definition. The former president of one of our national peers described the evolution of his university from a state university, to a state-related university, to a state-located university. Another speaks openly about a "remote relationship to the state in which it is located."

Meeting with our deans and vice chancellors last week, I was most pleased to hear a robust commitment to Carolina's status as a public university—a proudly public university. In fact, the question was asked, "Is our vision of being the leading public university compatible with the idea of being 'the university of the people?'" Are the two reconcilable?

I shall argue that they are; that they must be. But I will admit that this is a critical question that we dare not leave unanswered. It speaks to the charge that we hear now and then around the state that Carolina is arrogant and has lost touch with the people. These are the people who looked to Carolina when Edward Kidder Graham said, "Send us your problems." And Albert Coates and Howard Odum and countless other faculty and staff in Chapel Hill responded by shaping their research and service agendas around the needs of the people of North Carolina. UNC was already an engaged university, emerging as the flagship of the South. In describing the South of the 1940s, 50s and 60s in his book, *Speak Now Against the Day*, John Egerton wrote: "The single most glowing exception to broad-based mediocrity in the Southern academic world was the University of North Carolina at Chapel

Hill. The university acquired a level of independence and quality that kept it in the front rank of public and private schools in the region."[3]

We must balance our vision of excellence with our history and tradition of engagement and service to North Carolina. This is part of our genetic code, a core value. We must be, at the same time, a great global university and a university that is grounded with a strong sense of place, remembering that we are owned by the people of North Carolina. Indeed, the excellence and prominence we seek is for the benefit of the people, not ourselves.

I have said many times that our vision is more a journey than a destination. There is never an end-point in the quest for excellence. All institutions are constantly in a state of flux. Stasis is impossible. A university is either improving in quality, or it is slipping. We need to measure our relative standing with our peers, and then mark our progress (or lack of progress) year by year, looking for positive movement. What we are seeking is a dynamic sense of momentum and progress in the areas that we decide are the critical measures of excellence.

In October, we expect to see a first draft of the academic plan, which has been developed over the past several months by a broad cross-section of faculty. This plan will guide the five-year financial planning process I described earlier. It will also provide a general outline for more precise discussions about our collective aspirations for excellence in the College of Arts and Sciences, and the professional schools. We will ask each dean to make presentations to the Board of Trustees in the coming months about areas of strength and future potential. That process will be very important as we define and articulate the strengths that will carry Carolina forward in the future.

At our recent retreat with the deans and vice chancellors, we considered measures of excellence in several broad categories. In each case, our intention will be to measure and track UNC's performance against that of the major peer institutions with which we compete—the Association of American Universities and specifically those top four institutions generally regarded as superior to us in most categories—Berkeley, UCLA, Michigan, and in undergraduate measures, Virginia. In each of these areas we should focus both on the point on the scale for each measure as compared to our peers over time, and on the gradient or direction of the line.

Students, the Quality of the Learning Environment, and Outcomes
First, we should measure over time the quality of students attracted to UNC, using metrics that are very familiar to us. More importantly, we should assess, measure and compare with data from AAU peers, the quality of the learning environment at Chapel Hill, measuring such things as the percentage of students in freshman seminars or senior capstone seminars, the percentage of students engaged in study abroad or undergraduate research, for example. We must continue to pay attention to what our students are telling us in satisfaction surveys of advising, for example, and track that over time. And we must also constantly strive to build upon our recent impressive gains in improving the racial and ethnic diversity of our student population, which continues to grow both in number and in quality of preparation.

And finally, we should track the outcomes of a Carolina education, again measuring and tracking our own record against that of our peers. Beyond the obvious (graduation and retention rates), we should look at the number of significant awards earned by our graduates and their placement into prestigious graduate and professional programs. Similar measures should be created for graduate and professional degree programs themselves, of course, and we shall ask every program to tailor measures to fit their individual programs.

Improvement in any of these key areas will bring resource requirements, and that is why we must connect our aspirations with the goals of the Carolina First Campaign. For example, I propose that we double the size of the Honors Program, already one of the best and most accessible in the country. With a new endowment of $25 million, we could add the necessary faculty lines to support this expansion of the Honors Program, increasing our yield of high-ability students, and, at the same time, adding faculty to high priority areas of the College.

We should recognize that these various aspects of student measurement constitute a reinforcing feedback loop. Improving the quality of the educational experience we offer means we will attract even better students in the future. Attracting more students who are well-prepared for college will, in turn, enhance the intellectual climate across the campus.

Certain aspects of university life are intangible and not measurable. A critical aspect of excellence is the degree to which the students at this university grow not only in knowledge but also in character and personal ethics. From our earliest days, the concept of honor has been at the core of a Carolina education.[4] The Honor Code, and the history at Carolina of a student-administered system of academic discipline and justice, is one of our most cherished traditions.

Convinced that this hallowed tradition was in great need of reform and rejuvenation, last year I appointed a special task force to review the student judicial system. That committee, chaired by Professor Marilyn Yarbrough in the School of Law, has now made its recommendations. The Committee on Student Conduct will solicit input from the Carolina community before sending proposed legislation to Student Congress and Faculty Council. The cynics are saying that the congress and council will talk reform to death. I challenge us all to prove the cynics wrong.

Let us resolve to return the concept of honor to the center of the stage. It is clear that we have some major work to do. Moreover, let us find a way to make our commitment to honor measurable, so that year by year we can hold ourselves accountable to a rising standard of performance.

In this discussion of students and learning, I have focused on undergraduate education. However, similar and parallel issues apply at the graduate and professional level. I call on every graduate and professional program to apply the same rising standards of admissions and acceptance, quality of experience, and measurable outcomes.

The Faculty

Let us turn now to the faculty whose collective excellence defines a great university. There are many quantifiable measures of the quality of a university's faculty: the number of those elected to the national academies; the number receiving significant national awards; peer-reviewed external funding and publications; all of which can be benchmarked against our peers.

Faculty compensation is an area where UNC has struggled to keep up. Our situation is complicated by the fact that our competition is not just the other great public universities, but the well-endowed private institutions as well. Coupled with woefully inadequate benefit packages, we find ourselves each year in a mounting struggle to fend off raids for our best people from other institutions. We are now tracking these contests—about half of which we are winning—and the cost of the retention packages in the successful cases, as well as the known salary gaps in those instances where we were unsuccessful in countering offers. It is, in fact, a mark of excellence when the most distinguished universities in the country want our faculty. As one dean remarked last week, we want to have faculty that the University of Chicago also wants. But we need the resources to match Chicago's.

Ultimately, our goal of establishing 200 new endowed chairs for faculty through the Carolina First Campaign will be a critical building block in attracting and retaining the very best faculty. But that success will not lessen our resolve to continue making our case in Raleigh to fund pay raises for both faculty and staff. In the recent past, a major source of funds for faculty salary increases has been campus-initiated tuition increases. The state must recognize its responsibility in this regard. We will do our part in raising private funds and in recommending moderate increases in tuition, but we must be mindful of our commitment to access. We cannot, should not, must not place the full burden of faculty salary increases on our students.

We must also recognize that we have some serious work to do internally on faculty issues. Very shortly, we shall receive recommendations from a task force regarding appointments, promotions and tenure. These are the most important decisions we make. We need to be certain that we have a rigorous system of peer review and standards and procedures that are consistently applied across the university. I do not believe that is the case today.

Research and Graduate Education

Chapel Hill continues to make incredible strides with regard to growth in peer-reviewed funded research, which increased in 2001 to $438 million, up more than 17% over the previous year. A major factor was National Institutes of Health (NIH) funding, which continues to rise steadily. Last year all five of UNC's health affairs schools—dentistry, medicine, nursing, pharmacy, and public health—ranked within the top 25 of public and private schools according to the NIH. Three of those professional schools were in the top 5. We also broke into the top 20 universities receiving science and technology funding from the National Science Foundation, the only such university in North Carolina so designated. Our research numbers this year are even more impressive. Total awards for 2002 exceeded $488 million, an 11-percent increase. This recent growth in research funding corresponds directly with the legislature's decision in 1998 permitting the university to retain and reinvest the reimbursements of the costs of research. What a return on investment! Let me repeat those numbers: in 2001, $438 million. In 2002, $488 million. I suggest a round of applause for a great and distinguished faculty.

In 2001, we made a significant investment in genomic sciences. Since then, we have assembled a world-class team of the best scientists in the world. The School of Public Health was designated by the U.S. Centers for Disease Control and Prevention as one of the nation's three centers of excellence along with the universities of Michigan and Washington.

We continue to build cooperative programs with Duke and NC State. For example, we are developing a new Ph.D. in biomedical engineering with NC State, building on the strength in science and medicine at Chapel Hill and engineering at State. We have just established a new Triangle National Lithography Center, with significant investments from both Carolina and NC State, which will focus on green manufacturing methods and nanoscale structures. The real beneficiary of this new center will be North Carolina's economy, with the stimulus of new business and job creation.

We have additional strengths within UNC-Chapel Hill that will eventually lead to the development of our own new campus at Carolina North. As a first step in that direction, I propose the creation of a new Institute for Advanced Materials, Nanoscience and Technology, building on existing strengths already present in the departments of chemistry, physics, computer science, and other units engaged in this critical technology.

Some will argue that we cannot afford new initiatives in the current environment. I would respond that, while we must be very judicious in taking on new projects, we cannot afford not to build on our strengths to be the very best that we can be. I think we should all agree on one thing—that we will start nothing that we are not willing to support sufficiently to make it a top-10 program within a reasonable period of time. We must be willing to pull the plug of life support on new programs that fail to meet that threshold.

We should not only invest in big science, in programs that span the traditional disciplines, we should do the same in the humanities, the social sciences, and the professions.

Our library is one of our great strengths and we must continue to build it. And somewhere in this audience is Ben Jones. This morning Ben brought me a copy of the 1612 first edition of the King James Bible for the Rare Book Collection in Wilson Library. He bought this book at an auction in Hendersonville, North Carolina, outbidding all the other bidders. Finally, when he announced that the book was going to the University of North Carolina, they broke into applause, stamping their feet. I said to Ben, "Either the room was filled with Tar Heels, or they were relieved that, at last, the infidels in Chapel Hill were going to have a Bible."

I am enormously proud of our social scientists who have teamed up with the Chinese Academy of Social Science to make UNC the lead institution in the study of the impact of the Olympic Games in the urbanization of China. We have invested in the Center for the Study of the American South, and Chapel Hill is once again the "go-to" place for study of this region.

The School of Law recently created a new Center for Civil Rights, which is committed to the study of civil rights and social justice, especially in the American South, and is directed by Julius Chambers, a UNC law graduate and one of the nation's great champions of civil rights. This new center just hosted with Harvard and other partners a major conference examining the re-segregation of Southern schools.

The Kenan-Flagler Business School has launched its new OneMBA program, linking it with partners around the world for a truly global program in executive education.

Next month, we shall open with pride the new Institute for Arts and Humanities, built entirely with private support. Long one of the jewels of the Carolina culture, the institute will now be housed in a jewel box of a facility. Later in the fall, we shall unveil the plan for the arts common, a truly visionary plan that will provide the footprint for an orderly build-out of new and renovated facilities for the arts spanning the next 50 years.

Conclusion

This is the vision of a great university that has captured the imagination of those who love Chapel Hill. But does this vision matter to the people of North Carolina? And why should it?

The answer, I hope, is obvious. As a proudly public university, we should mark our progress not only by measuring ourselves against our peers. We must also judge ourselves by what we contribute to North Carolina. This commitment is best expressed through our engagement with the state, a mission that transcends public service, linking our research and creativity to the felt needs of the state.

I want to go further and suggest, in conclusion, an even more profound relationship with the people that goes back to the very 18th-century conception of the university. Peter Gomes, the Plummer Professor of Christian Morals and Minister to the Memorial Church at Harvard, in his new book,

The Good Life, quotes a Harvard student, who asked, in despair over some of Harvard's own policies and actions, "Why can't Harvard be both great and good at the same time?"[5]

Let me re-phrase that question for us: Can Carolina be both great and good at the same time? That suggests a university with a moral compass, a university with a sense of public virtue. As I study the history of this place, that is the characteristic that shines through in our greatest moments. From our earliest days through the recent past, Chapel Hill has been both a rock of stability and an agent of change always characterized by a culture of civility and humanity. The words of the prophet Micah are inscribed on Gerrard Hall, the second chapel erected on this campus in 1822: "What does the Lord require of thee, but to do justice, to love mercy, and to walk humbly with thy God."

We can pursue a vision of excellence—of being America's leading public university—and not lose the faith of the people whose university this is, if we maintain that spirit of doing justice, loving kindness, in a spirit of humility. Excellence without pretension.

There is no standard set of metrics for that kind of university. But we who love this place know the feel, the smell, the sound of such a university. Thomas Wolfe called it magical. Frank Porter Graham talked about the music in the air.

As we begin a new academic year, we need to remind ourselves that each year we must re-create this culture of excellence and engagement, of creativity and commitment, of being rather than seeming; doing justice, loving kindness, and walking in humility. Grounded with that moral compass, we can shine as a true light on the hill. The brightest star of all.

Notes

1. Moeser, James. "State of the University Address." Chapel Hill, N.C. Delivered September 5, 2001

2. Coffin, William Sloane. *The Heart is a Little to the Left: Essays on Public Morality*. University Press of New England. Dartmouth College, 1999, p. 3

3. Egerton, John. *Speak Now Against the Day: The Generation Before the Civil Rights Movement in the South*. University of North Carolina Press, 1995, p. 130.

4. Graham, Edward Kidder, "The College and Human Need," an address before

the student body at the opening of the University of North Carolina, September, 1915. Published in: *Education and Citizenship and Other Papers by Edward Kidder Graham*. New York and London: G.P. Putnam's Sons, 1919, pp. 137–47.

5. Gomes, Peter J. *The Good Life: Truths That Last in Times of Need*. Harper San Francisco, 2002, p. 23.

2003 STATE OF THE UNIVERSITY ADDRESS

The University of North Carolina at Chapel Hill
October 12, 2003

*T*HE 2003 ADDRESS WAS *not delivered until University Day, October 12, but it makes no mention of another swirling controversy over the reading assignment for first year students, Barbara Ehrenreich's* Nickel and Dimed: On (Not) Getting By in America, *a book about low-income hourly wage earners in America. Again, UNC was attacked from the right, this time for having students read a book described as a "socialist rant." The controversy was not really over, but I concluded that I shouldn't focus on it. So, it went without reference.*

North Carolina was experiencing in a very existential sense the loss of manufacturing in the textile and furniture industries, which had long been engines of employment in the state. I mentioned the closing of the Pillowtex plant in Kannapolis, one of the largest of these plants that closed with the loss of thousands of jobs.

Because of the state's economic downturn, UNC had gone for several years with little or no salary increases for faculty and staff. Faculty retention was at a crisis state—with the College of Arts and Sciences losing 60 percent of the faculty for whom retention efforts were made. The Carolina First Campaign was beginning to have some real success with fund raising for endowed chairs and scholarships, but my job in 2003 was to keep hope alive on the campus.

The most important announcement in this address was the creation of the Carolina Covenant, which initially promised a debt-free education to all stu-

dents admitted from families earning 150 percent of the federal poverty level. (The following year, we raised that to 200 percent of the poverty level.)

JUST A FEW WEEKS ago, the vice chancellors and deans participated in a planning retreat led by Dr. James Duderstadt, president emeritus of the University of Michigan. This is his assessment of the state of our world, in expressly Dickensian terms:

"In many ways, these do indeed seem like both the best of times and the worst of times for higher education. Universities are increasingly seen as key sources to the new knowledge and educated citizens so necessary for a knowledge-driven society. After two decades of eroding public support at the state and federal level, there is an increasing call for reinvestment in higher education. [...] Yet there is great unease on our campuses," Duderstadt continues. "Throughout society we see erosion in support of important university commitments such as academic freedom, tenure, broad access, and racial diversity. Even the concept of higher education as a public good is being challenged, as society increasingly sees a college education as an individual benefit determined by values of the marketplace rather than the broader needs of a democratic society. The faculty feels increasing stress, fearing an erosion in public support [...] and being pulled out of the classroom and the laboratory by the demands of grantsmanship."[1]

As we reflect on our own situation in North Carolina, and as we glance over our shoulders at the difficulties faced by public universities in the other states, we can see many signs of trouble—a national economy that is less than robust with signs of an economic recovery that may be accompanied by continued loss of jobs to other parts of the world.

To that we must factor in the incredible commitment of the people of North Carolina to support public higher education, as reflected in the voters' decision to support, by an overwhelming margin, the Higher Education Bond Issue in 2000, and in this most recent budget cycle, the strong efforts of Governor Mike Easley and the General Assembly to shield our state's universities from the full force of budget cuts to state government. We enjoy a far greater level of support historically in North Carolina than almost every other state, and when we compare our budget cuts with those meted out in other states, we know we have much for which we should be thankful.

This year we adopted Carolina's academic plan, which maps out the priorities that should guide us in our day-to-day and year-to-year decisions supporting our vision of becoming America's leading public university. The plan acknowledges that, although state support remains essential to the university's future, it has steadily declined as a percentage of our total budget as other sources have grown faster. State appropriations account for a quarter of our operating budget—down from more than 30 percent just a few years ago.

At Carolina, we are generating new revenue sources to help meet some of our most pressing needs. We rely more today on our faculty's skills in attracting research funding, as well as on generous private giving. However, we cannot assume that research grants will continue to rise at the same 10 to 12 percent levels we have seen in the past as increases for federal funding begin to level off. Our progress in private fund raising will depend, at least in part, on the nation's economy. Further, we cannot predict how North Carolina's budget difficulties will affect our campus.

While Duderstadt's assessment of the current trends is accurate, I think that North Carolina is a special case. The loss of jobs in the manufacturing sector will hit our state harder than many others. The Pillowtex plant closing and the thousands of textile jobs lost in the Kannapolis area underscores the need for economic transformation. Research universities can lead in creating a knowledge-based economy, and in a state that is so dependent upon manufacturing, we must lead.

In that light, one of the most pressing challenges facing Carolina is this: Can we remain true today to two centuries of commitment to public higher education and, at the same time, aspire to be the nation's leading public university? What does it mean to be "the University of the People" in the 21st century? Or, as I asked in last year's address, can Carolina be both great and good? Can we achieve excellence while honoring our tradition of doing what is right? Later in this address, I will announce an exciting new initiative that will help us answer some of these questions.

The Academic Plan: A Roadmap for Future Success

First, I want to explore some additional context provided by the academic plan, intended to guide our decision making over the next five years. Among the plan's priorities are for the university to provide the strongest possible academic experience for our undergraduate students.

What distinguishes Carolina from our major national peers—UC Berkeley, Michigan, and UCLA? We, to a greater extent than our peers, have retained a special blended culture of learning and discovery, with faculty who are involved in research, often at the cutting edge, but still deeply engaged in teaching. Our recent investments in improving the undergraduate experience, including first-year seminars and the Office of Undergraduate Research, are paying powerful dividends in the lives of our undergraduates. The Honors Program provides another fundamental example of what is right with our undergraduate education. It is recognized nationally for its accessibility to all undergraduates eager for the challenge of an honors experience — students working with faculty in small-group settings. As part of the Carolina First Campaign, we aim to double the size of this program. A $25 million endowment would create 14 new faculty positions in key departments in the College of Arts and Sciences. That would create enough new honors sections for another 150 students in each entering class. This alone would dramatically increase the yield of high-ability students enrolling at Carolina.

First-year seminars are a critical component of the excellence we provide for undergraduates. I call on us to commit the resources so that every first-year student can enroll in at least one of these seminars.

Our four newest student residence halls on south campus are designed to integrate learning and living, recognizing that today's students tell us that they learn best in small cells of students working together outside of class. Let us increase the number of seminars and discussion groups being offered in the residence halls themselves, really integrating living and learning. This is another strong recommendation from the academic plan that is important as we see the campus master plan come to life.

The academic plan also calls for sustained but modest enrollment growth as Carolina does its share to educate the rising number of high school graduates in North Carolina. This was our commitment to the citizens who supported the bond referendum. Every year for the next five years, we will admit more first-year North Carolina resident students.

At the same time, the University of North Carolina system is considering a plan articulated by President Broad that recognizes that the current 18-percent cap on out-of-state freshmen may impose a barrier to our enrolling more academically outstanding students. We strongly support this proposal to adjust the cap on out-of-state enrollment because it can help stem the "brain drain" leading many of North Carolina's best and brightest to attend out-of-state colleges that enroll more geographically diverse student bodies. Of the North Carolina students admitted to Carolina who decline our offer, between 43 and 51 percent of them leave our state. President Broad's plan would permit us to exempt from the current cap 40 to 50 National Merit Scholars, named merit scholarship holders, and valedictorians from other states. By doing so, we can create a more geographically varied and more intellectually stimulating environment that will be more attractive to these exceptional North Carolinians as well. Several studies show that those states that attract and retain intellectual capital will be the most successful in creating the knowledge-based economies that produce new jobs.

This is good public policy for North Carolina. Our vision of becoming the nation's leading public university is for the greater benefit of the people of North Carolina. If our state is to flourish in a 21st-century world economy, it must have an excellent global university whose students experience the world, rubbing shoulders with students from other backgrounds and cultures.

Each of these initiatives will help us in achieving excellence, in becoming great so we can better serve the people. But how do we ensure that we are also good—that is, supporting our traditional core values of being the "University of the People," of standing for justice and equity?

The Carolina Covenant: Connecting with Core Values

Today, American higher education is engaged in a national conversation about the affordability of a college education. Tuition, fees, and other costs are rising; the unmet needs of low-income students and their families are growing. Too often, these trends send a message that attending college is not possible, particularly to prospective first-generation students. The time is right again for Carolina to lead, as we did two years ago in taking the bold step of eliminating binding early-decision admissions.

Today, I am proud to announce a new commitment to access for our most needy students that we call the Carolina Covenant, a college-financing agreement between the University of North Carolina at Chapel Hill and low-income students from across the state and nation. The Carolina Covenant promises to our most needy students the opportunity to graduate from this University without any debt. Here is how it works:

First, this opportunity will be available to students who are admitted to Carolina, qualify for federal student aid, and come from a family with an income at or below 150 percent of the federal poverty level, indexed by family size. Using those criteria, that means a student from a family of four with an income of approximately $28,000 in 2002–03 would qualify. The University will meet 100 percent of this student's financial need through a combination of federal, state, campus-based, privately funded grants and scholarships, as well as his or her participation in the federal work-study job program.

We know of no other public university—and only Princeton among the privates—that has taken a comparable step to guarantee access to higher education. The covenant begins with next year's entering class and will be phased in over four years. Because we meet 100 percent of the financial need of our students, this is a program that is now within our reach as a result of the state's increased commitment to need-based aid and our own success in private fund-raising.

The covenant sends a powerful message about Carolina's core values, of its commitment to access as well as excellence. It expresses who we are. We are America's first public university, and these values are in our genetic code. The covenant embodies what we proclaim to be: "The University of the People." To paraphrase the late Governor Terry Sanford, it says to people of limited means everywhere, "If you have the will, we have the way."[2]

Great ideas come from great people, and I want to acknowledge the commitment and vision of Shirley Ort, Associate Provost and Director of Scholarships and Student Aid, and Jerry Lucido, Vice Provost for Enrollment Management and director of admissions, in crafting this new initiative.

Another core value at Carolina is honor and integrity, which we are celebrating with a yearlong emphasis, following the first revisions in 35 years of the Honor Code last year. I want to thank Judith Wegner for her leadership on this issue, as well as Student Attorney General Jonathan Slain and many others who have worked to restore the culture of honor on this campus. Now, more than ever, our students need to draw upon the ethical code of behavior, which they learn here, as they prepare to enter a world facing so many challenges. I encourage us all to participate in these worthy activities this year.

Let me also emphasize, as does the academic plan, the University's resolve in seeking continuous improvement with respect to diversity. I was so proud last spring with the response of our Law School faculty supporting the University of Michigan in its landmark affirmative action case. The U.S. Supreme Court's decision reflected our faculty's views about the special role a public university has in developing future leaders. The court also affirmed our own admissions practices, which have served us so well in building a diverse and highly qualified student body. While we have achieved much, we must not become complacent. There is still much to do.

Interdisciplinary Research and Strategic Opportunities

In the area of research, the academic plan identifies five broad interdisciplinary themes of strategic opportunity: (1) biological, medical, and technology sciences; (2) fine arts, humanities, and social sciences; (3) global citizenship; (4) social problem-solving; and (5) ethics, leadership, and public life. Within each of these themes, our University has achieved notable areas of recognized excellence, others in which we are building strength based on new investments, and still others that promise multi-unit capacity to address pressing issues facing North Carolina, the nation, and the world.

We must target available resources to the academic plan's designated areas of strength and potential, adopting the principle of expansion by substitution, recognizing that in an era of constrained resources we may be able to take on new programs only by shedding old ones. This is not something that comes easily, but we have reached a time when we cannot avoid it if we are going to continue to grow, improve, and not slip behind our peers. We must be rigorous in our internal review and evaluation of graduate programs, particularly doctoral programs, and willing to eliminate those programs that are not nationally competitive or critical to our mission.

We have made substantial progress in convincing state policymakers of the importance of retaining all of our facility and administration reimbursements from the federal government, funds commonly known as overhead receipts. Because we have reinvested these funds back into research facilities and infrastructure, our research funding has risen steadily, by 10 percent to more than $537 million last year.

Collaborative academic and research partnerships are another key to our future success, and this is another area of emphasis in the academic plan. One example is our role in a consortium that was just awarded a $45 million federal grant for biodefense. Some of our leading infectious diseases and immunology experts will work with colleagues at Duke University and other Southeastern institutions to develop the next generation of vaccines, drugs, and diagnostic tests against emerging infections such as SARS and to defend against organisms that could be used in a bioterrorist attack.

At the same time, we continue to build upon close ties with North Carolina State University, most recently through a joint graduate degree program in biomedical engineering that began this fall. We need to keep strengthening relationships with other UNC system campuses—especially North Carolina Central University here in the Triangle—as well as others across the state.

Beyond the state and the nation, we want to extend Carolina's global presence, research, and teaching. Area studies and global health are among the interdisciplinary areas of strategic opportunity noted in the academic plan. We aim to build and integrate global issues and perspectives into our undergraduate curricula, graduate and professional student experiences, and the overall research enterprise. We just took an important step in coordinating these international activities with the creation of a new position, Associate Provost for International Affairs, made possible by a generous private gift.

Investing in Carolina's Human Capital

The most critical investment we have to make is in our own people, both staff and faculty. Outstanding students and impressive buildings by themselves do not help transform an already great American research university. But, when combined with a faculty and staff of the caliber we have and want at Carolina, we can realize our vision for the future.

To achieve those goals, we must work more diligently among ourselves, within the UNC system, and with our state's elected leadership, including the General Assembly, to address vital compensation and benefit issues that are adversely affecting our ability to retain and attract the best faculty and staff.

The university's exceptional staff are full partners with the faculty in many of the core activities of the campus. Many staff have gone three years or more without any meaningful salary increases while facing rising cost of living—17 percent for health insurance just this year. Regrettably, we are losing some of our best staff as a result, and we cannot permit that trend to continue.

While we have funded modest salary increases for faculty from campus-based tuition increases, we have not been able to provide central campus resources for staff salary increases. I want to commend those departments and units that have reallocated their own resources to recognize excellence with in-range salary adjustments for qualified employees. But we must address across the campus this urgent concern about compensation and work with the university system in taking this message to the General Assembly.

And the issue is not just salary. Our benefits packages are not competitive when compared with our public and private peers. This is true for faculty and staff. We attach a very high priority to this concern.

We are examining a host of issues through the Chancellor's Task Force for a Better Workplace, which I am co-chairing with Tommy Griffin. The task force is working hard to identify areas where all of us can improve the quality of the workplace for our employees. I expect our final report to be completed later this fall.

Now let me focus on some of the most serious issues facing the faculty. For several years we have been charting our success in faculty retention, and here we are beginning to see very troubling signs. From 1991 until 2000, we successfully retained 60 percent of the College faculty who received offers from other institutions for whom we made counter-offers. In the first two years of this decade, we succeeded in about half of those cases in the College. Last year, however, the percentage of losses in the College climbed to 60 percent, while across the university at large it was even higher. This is a trend that we cannot allow to continue.

We must convince the state that regular appropriations for merit salary increases are essential, lest we create a culture in which our best faculty are shopping for offers as the only means of improving their individual situations. We could quickly lose the essence of what has made Carolina great—a real community of scholars who invested their lives in a deep and lasting commitment not only to their scholarship, but to the community itself.

Recognizing that the quality of the faculty is the key to excellence, the leadership of the Carolina First Campaign has rallied around the need to support resources for the recruitment and retention of outstanding faculty as the campaign's number one objective. Our donors are responding. The campaign has secured commitments approaching $1.1 billion toward its $1.8 billion goal by 2007. Campaign funds have created 105 new distinguished professorships, more than half our total goal of 200.

The campaign also seeks to provide research and program support for faculty, as well as for the bricks and mortar essential to their work. Every campaign goal strengthens in one way or another the over-arching objective of improving faculty support. We have secured funds to establish more than 350 new scholarships and graduate fellowships; our goal is 1,000. These help us bring the brightest and best students to Carolina, creating the stimulating intellectual climate that draws and retains great faculty. They, in turn, attract great students, creating a reinforcing loop that builds excellence.

Second in importance to the human infrastructure is our physical infrastructure. We are making great progress with our capital construction program using the higher education bonds, overhead receipts from research grants, and private gifts. The science complex, the largest construction project in our history, and research facilities in several health science schools will put cutting-edge facilities and equipment in the hands of our faculty and students for research and discovery. The Global Education Center is another key project bringing a growing variety of international activities in schools and units together in one physical location.

Engagement: A Cornerstone of a Proudly Public Tradition

Carolina is an engaged university. In his inaugural address in 1915, President Edward Kidder Graham declared that "the state university is the instrument of democracy for realizing all [these] high and healthful aspirations of the state."[3]

The University transforms people's lives each and every day across North Carolina. Earlier this year, in Windsor, North Carolina, I saw a remarkable health-education success story connected with our North Carolina Breast Cancer Screening Program, led by faculty in our School of Public Health and based in the Lineberger Comprehensive Cancer Center. Volunteers are at the heart of this program for women in eastern North Carolina dedicated to reducing late-stage diagnosis of breast and cervical cancer in older African-American women. Over the past decade, this federally supported research program has succeeded in bringing more at-risk women in for mammograms.

Each of our professional schools has a reach that fully meets Edward Kidder Graham's vision of the campus being coterminous with the borders of the state. Whether it is one of the five health science schools, or journalism and mass communication, law, business, social work, or information and library science, or government, Carolina reaches all 100 counties of North Carolina and beyond. We are dealing with the real problems and opportunities of the state and the region.

The College is equally engaged. As just one example, I cite the nationally recognized efforts of Biology Professor Skip Bollenbacher's team in collaborating on innovative science education and distance-learning programs. This excellent work is occurring in the public schools and through a consortium joining us with seven historically minority colleges and universities across the state. Those projects include the highly successful Traveling Education Science Laboratory and the Partnership for Minority Advancement in the Biomolecular Sciences. Through them, Carolina is promoting the promise of science careers to the next generation of leaders and helping fellow faculty more effectively teach the latest science from new fields. UNC-Chapel Hill is sharing expertise and technology with other students and teachers who would not otherwise have access to this knowledge. It is but one example of how the University can help North Carolina prepare the science-literate workforce our state will need in the future.

Town-Gown Relations

Engagement begins at home. The University is now turning its attention to working together with the Town of Chapel Hill on maintaining Franklin Street and the downtown business district.

Franklin Street is not only the vibrant heart of Chapel Hill, it is the front door to our campus. We share with the town a vital interest in its economic and aesthetic vitality as a destination in its own right. Our physical plan for the arts common, as well as our plans for a more ambitious program of presenting the performing arts, can help make downtown a destination. The University is committed to partnering productively with the town to help local businesses thrive downtown.

As the University grows physically, we must continue to be sensitive to the impact our development has on the local community. Let me shine some light on one little-known example. Last fall, as part of our commitment to traffic mitigation, we launched a commuter alternatives program, which provides incentives to commuters to use transit, park and ride, bike or walk. Our goal was 750 participants, which we exceeded by 250 percent. Those results earned the program a major national honor—designation as a 2003 Best Workplaces for Commuters by the Environmental Protection Agency and the U.S. Department of Transportation. That award speaks to the University's commitment to being a responsible employer and community member.

Let me acknowledge the leadership of Chapel Hill Mayor Kevin Foy in working with Trustees "Stick" Williams and Roger Perry in guiding recent discussions about the University's plans and in affirming our desire to be an excellent neighbor. Their skills helped move us forward. We expect and look forward to a similar collaborative approach to guide future discussions about our plans to develop Carolina North.

Conclusion

After more than three years as your chancellor, I can tell you that Carolina remains as magical a place to me as it did from the moment I set foot on this beautiful campus. The people in this room today, and the other members of the Carolina family who are not here, are responsible for whatever success we enjoy. Your dedication to excellence—to students learning, teachers teaching, and all of us serving the people of North Carolina and beyond—is truly inspirational.

Despite our current short-term obstacles, I am confident about Carolina's future. My optimism is grounded in your dedication. I place a great deal of trust—and faith—in the history of this place, the light on the hill, and a shared sense that it is our destiny to succeed. The people of Carolina have always found ways to do the remarkable, the right, the just thing. That is a characteristic that will forever mark this University.

Today, we are translating the vision of those leaders who came before us and the language of two centuries of commitment to public higher education into new ways of thinking about being public, committed to access and public service. We are doing so while pursuing our vision of being a world-class university. Let us resolve to be both great and good; to lead and to serve; to build both the mind and the spirit; advancing human knowledge and human values; that we shall be—for the 21st century—as we were meant to be, The University of the People.[4]

Notes

1. Duderstadt, James J. *A University for the 21st Century*. Ann Arbor, Mich.: The University of Michigan Press, 2000, p. 319

2. Sanford, Terry. "Special Insights from the Hill: A Bilateral Perspective." *Educational Record*, 1990, 71, 13–14

3. Snider, William D. *Light on the Hill: A History of The University of North Carolina at Chapel Hill*. Chapel Hill and London, The University of North Carolina Press, 1992, p. 160.

4. Kuralt, Charles. Opening Ceremony Remarks, Bicentennial Observance, Chapel Hill, N.C. Delivered October 12, 1993. Following is the famous description: "What binds us to this place as no other? It is not the well or the bell or the stone walls, or the crisp October nights or our memory of dogwood blooming.... No, our love for this place is based on the fact that it is as it was meant to be—The University of the People."

2004 STATE OF THE UNIVERSITY ADDRESS

The University of North Carolina at Chapel Hill
September 29, 2004

*T*HIS ADDRESS STANDS IN *strong contrast to the address one year earlier, which was marked by economic downturn, plant closings, and negative faculty retention. I had begun to hit my stride as Chancellor.*

In the spring of 2004, we began "Carolina Connects," an ambitious program of visiting the communities across the state, taking the story of Carolina's relevance to every region of North Carolina, letting our faculty and students explain why their work was affecting the quality of life for all North Carolinians. This was a carefully planned campaign to build public support for the University, with the hope and belief that this would translate into legislative support. This program was more than a public relations campaign—it issued from the deep wells of Carolina's core values. The faculty and staff rallied to support it because they knew it was genuine.

Improving working conditions for staff was an important issue in 2003–04. The Task Force for a Better Workplace, which I co-chaired with Tommy Griffin, the chair of the Employee Forum, resulted in some concrete actions which, I believe, improved the work environment for staff and helped morale.

The General Assembly was much kinder to UNC in 2004. Funds for the North Carolina Cancer Hospital were appropriated. We were allowed to use campus-based tuition to increase faculty salaries, and we began to turn the tide of negative faculty retention. It gave me enormous pleasure to report that, for the first time in recent memory, there was not a single recorded vote on the overhead receipts we receive from research grants and contracts.

Finally, in this address I laid out for the campus seven over-arching priorities that the Trustees and I agreed upon over a summer retreat. At last, we had an agenda for progress.

Carolina Connects

A leading public university is an engaged university. It is a university that always puts its state first. I have traveled across North Carolina, visiting people in small communities and big cities from every corner of our state.

These visits show the connections between the University and the people of North Carolina, focusing on the work our faculty, staff, and students do to improve people's lives in all 100 counties. This University truly serves North Carolina every day in meaningful, relevant ways. In short, Carolina connects.

Carolina Connects has been well received. My travels have highlighted different areas of our work in public education, health care, and economic development. Conversations with community leaders, elected officials, alumni, parents, and others have been invaluable.

Let me mention just a few of the wonderful people I have met from Carolina and in our state's communities:

- Jill Fitzgerald, a School of Education professor, taught for a year at Siler City Elementary School, which, in many ways, mirrors our state. The school is dealing with an influx of immigrants who do not speak English as a first language. Jill says her experience in that Siler City classroom changed about 80 percent of what she had been teaching her own UNC students.
- Stuart Gold, a pediatric oncology specialist, epitomizes the roles that the Area Health Education Centers Program and UNC Health Care play across our state. Stuart's work at Wilmington's AHEC clinic helps save families the hardship of traveling to Chapel Hill for specialized care for their children that the local hospital cannot provide.
- Jin Yi Kwon, a dental student, has taught oral hygiene in a nursing home in Greensboro. She and the entire School of Dentistry's Class of 2007 have made a commitment to give four to eight hours each month to dental-related community service after they graduate.

- Rick Luettich and faculty at the Institute of Marine Sciences provide a direct economic benefit to Carteret County. Their work with Duke and other public–private partners contributes $127 million and more than 3,100 jobs to the county's economy. Their research informs us about our state's coast, considered the "world's largest wet lab" for marine and coastal environmental sciences.
- Anita Brown-Graham and Kevin FitzGerald of the School of Government and Jim Johnson of the Kenan-Flagler Business School assist Curtis Wynn in his efforts to spur economic development in northeastern North Carolina. Wynn, CEO of the Roanoke Electric Cooperative, hopes to reverse the historical economic challenges facing Bertie, Hertford, Gates, and Northampton counties.

Tomorrow, I will be in Kernersville with Mike Smith, dean of the School of Government, which is one of the jewels of our public service efforts, to participate in an economic development forum.

I have not hidden my ambition to help Chapel Hill be the leading public university in America. In some respects, we already are. But being the leading public university starts with fulfilling our mission close to home. This University must continue defining its research and public service agendas around the needs of the state. That is the definition of engagement. We work on real-world problems. We address local, as well as global, needs.

North Carolina needs our help. Improving health and public education. Creating jobs and contributing to the state's tax base. We have a great record of accomplishment, but we can and should do more. We recently appointed Jesse White, the former head of the Appalachian Regional Commission and the Southern Growth Policies Board, to lead our new Office of Economic and Business Development, which matches faculty and campus resources with statewide needs.

History shows why such efforts are so important. In the 1930s, Carolina Professor Howard Odum and UNC President Frank Porter Graham were at the cutting edge of social and economic reform in the South. In 1938 President Roosevelt asked Dr. Graham to chair an Advisory Committee on the Economic Conditions in the South, citing it as the nation's number one economic problem.[1]

In a recent essay, Law School Dean Gene Nichol wrote that the South is still the native home of American poverty. "It continues to sustain the highest poverty rate and the lowest average income of any section of the country. Nearly 14 percent of Southerners are poor and our income levels fall thousands of dollars below national averages." Nichol noted that North Carolina's median income is nearly $5,000 below the national average. "We are one of ten states whose median income actually fell from the year before—in our case by 4.4 percent."[2]

The Carolina Covenant: Reaching More Deserving Students

We recognize that access to higher education is the key to opportunity for a better life in a knowledge-based economy. That is why last year we launched the Carolina Covenant, a first for a major U.S. public university. The Carolina Covenant promises admitted students from low-income families that we will provide the full cost of their education so that they will not accumulate any debt.

This fall, we enrolled 225 Carolina Covenant Scholars. I met some of these students and their parents during my "Carolina Connects" visits. They are truly outstanding students who have impressed me with their academic credentials, their passions, and their interests. More than half of them are first-generation college students. They came to us highly prepared, with an average 4.21 GPA and 1,209 SAT score.

These are students and families who need our help. To put that into perspective, the average annual family income for a Carolina Covenant Scholar last year was $13,400. That is $400 less than what it costs a North Carolinian to attend the University this year. Recognizing that tuition accounts for only a third of the total cost of attendance, the Carolina Covenant goes even further to cover room and board, books, and other expenses.

Other universities, including Virginia, Maryland, Nebraska, and Harvard, have followed suit with their own programs to support high-ability, low-income students. And Brown University just joined that list.

Today, I am pleased to announce that we are raising the bar even higher to extend the reach of the Carolina Covenant. We are expanding the program for families from 150 percent of the federal poverty level to 200 percent. And that raises the threshold to cover a family of four with an annual income of about $37,000 or a single parent with a child who makes about $24,000. This adjustment begins with next fall's freshman class and will add an estimated 120 new Carolina Covenant Scholars.

These changes send an even stronger message about accessibility and the traditional commitment to opportunity at Carolina for qualified students—regardless of their ability to pay.

Our University is leading a true movement in American higher education. We hope our leadership last year in establishing the Carolina Covenant, and our increased commitment to the Covenant today, will challenge other universities to make similar investments to ensure affordability and access for deserving students.

This increased commitment is possible because of our trustees' policies emphasizing need-based aid and strong support from the State in funding financial aid as the cost of education rises. Increasingly, donors are pledging gifts—nearly $2.7 million to date—to support the Carolina Covenant through the Carolina First Campaign.

But what about the students from middle-class families? Do they bear the burden of higher tuition and costs of attendance? Not at this University. We meet the full need of middle-income students, with financial aid packages comprised of two-thirds grants and scholarships and one-third loans and work-study. And here is the proof: the average debt load among our graduating seniors who borrowed dropped from $13,700 in 2000 to $11,519 last year.

Our progress in this area stands in direct contrast to national trends, where the average for student debt loan doubled to about $17,000 in just a decade. Having made this massive commitment to need-based aid, we must now turn our attention to increasing the funding for non-need based merit scholarships, to make sure that we are competitive for the very best students who have offers from other institutions. We can do this without any compromise to our commitment to access and affordability.

Creating a Better Workplace

Over the past year, we have devoted a significant amount of attention to the needs of our staff through the Chancellor's Task Force for a Better Workplace, which I co-chaired with Tommy Griffin.

Let me list a few steps we are taking to implement the task force's recommendations:

- We established an ombuds office, which will provide confidential, informal, and neutral dispute resolution services to employees

with job-related concerns. We shall make two appointments in the coming weeks.
- Next fall, we will launch a pilot program for up to 10 employees with some college experience to earn undergraduate credit toward degrees as part-time students while working full time.
- We jumpstarted a computer loan initiative.
- We created a privately funded staff emergency loan program. I designated $25,000 of a recent estate gift to initiate this fund. And I have directed, with trustee approval, that another $200,000 from that gift remain in the endowment to support a scholarship program for children of our employees.
- We added another tier in the sliding-scale parking permit fee structure for employees making $25,000 or less.
- We expanded the C. Knox Massey Distinguished Service Awards, going from four to six recipients and increasing the monetary award in this, the 25th anniversary year of this program.

I am honored now to recognize those recipients, who represent the very best of an outstanding workforce: Sandra Caulberg, administrative officer, Office of University Counsel; David Godschalk, Stephen Baxter Professor Emeritus, Department of City and Regional Planning; Linda Naylor, administrative assistant, Office of the Executive Vice Chancellor and Provost; David Perry, executive associate dean for administration, School of Medicine; Elizabeth "Betsy" Taylor, student services manager, Academic Advising Program, College of Arts and Sciences; and Avon Seymore, grounds crew leader, Facilities Services Division.

Positive Accomplishments Build Momentum

Great things are happening at Carolina, and this past year has only added to the positive momentum. We just enrolled the most academically prepared freshman class in the University's history. We made major progress in a multi-year construction program that is bringing our campus master plan to life. Faculty research funding grew stronger. Enlightened alumni and friends demonstrated an extraordinary commitment by contributing generously to the Carolina First Campaign.

Against that backdrop, this past session of the General Assembly was highly successful for the University. For the first time in recent memory, there was not a single recorded vote on the overhead receipts we receive from research grants and contracts. Reductions in our budget were minimal and offset by funding for enrollment growth and salary increases.

Our legislators authorized $180 million to build a world-class hospital in Chapel Hill for cancer patients and their families from North Carolina and beyond. We have seen a 23-percent increase in the number of cancer patients coming here for care in the last five years. Over the next 30 years, the number of cancer cases in our state alone is expected to double. When completed, the new hospital will become the largest freestanding university cancer hospital in the Southeast and the clinical home for the UNC Lineberger Comprehensive Cancer Center, one of only 38 National Cancer Institute-designated centers.

We are grateful to Governor Easley and the General Assembly for this support. I also want to acknowledge the work of our own faculty, and most especially, the cancer patients themselves, who made the case so eloquently for this funding.

Seven University Priorities to Guide the Future

This summer, at our annual retreat, the Board of Trustees and I worked together on a list of the University's top priorities. I want to share them with you now. Each priority is keyed to our academic plan. Each builds upon and supports the others. And each priority addresses our overarching vision of being America's leading public university.

Strengthen Faculty Support

Our number one priority is strengthening faculty recruitment, retention, and development. We want to recruit and retain the very best minds and enhance the faculty culture that creates a lasting bond with the University and with North Carolina.

Let us focus for a moment on the faculty culture. This is one of our traditional strengths. We are a true community made up of faculty who are both esteemed scholars in their fields, as well as citizens of this community, engaged with each other across departmental lines, locally and across the state.

As our most senior faculty approach retirement, we must think about how we effectively re-create this culture with our new appointments. In an increasingly competitive environment, in which other institutions recognize the quality of our faculty by seeking to lure them away, we must give special attention to all the factors that make this an attractive place in which to live and work.

Our faculty chair, Judith Wegner, initiated an effort to examine all of these issues. The Office of Institutional Research recently completed a survey commissioned by the faculty leadership to gauge the forces that attract great faculty to Carolina, as well as what motivates people to stay, to put down roots, to become part of the community, and to build their careers here, as so many have done.

That is the culture we are determined to nurture and protect.

But we also need to understand the negative forces in our midst. Why do people entertain offers, and why do they leave? We know that stagnation in salary increases and benefits packages that are less than competitive have been a major factor, but what are the other, less tangible factors that can come into play?

Two years ago, we were alarmed that we lost two-thirds of the faculty receiving external offers whom we sought to retain. I am pleased that this past year we reversed that, thanks to efforts led by the provost and the deans to take appropriate pre-emptive steps to deal with critical areas of salary compression and equity. I am even more pleased that, this year, thanks to the General Assembly, and the campus- and school-based tuition revenue, we have begun to undo the destructive culture beginning to form that the only way to get ahead at Chapel Hill was to get an offer from someplace else.

Now, it takes more than one good rainfall to eliminate a major drought. And it will take several years of salary increases to put Chapel Hill back into parity with our major national peers.

Therefore, we will continue to make our case to the General Assembly for increases in salaries and benefits for faculty and staff. We will seek out other revenue sources we can generate ourselves, such as moderate increases in campus- or school-based tuition to support improved compensation for faculty and graduate teaching assistants. Private gifts will remain a priority, recognizing that we cannot look to the state alone to support the intense competition that Chapel Hill faces from well-endowed private institutions.

Through our Carolina First Campaign, we are making progress in building the quality of our great faculty. The campaign has secured nearly $211 million for faculty support—more than half of our recently revised goal of $400 million. Our steering committee increased that target a few months ago by $100 million because this issue is so critical. The major initiative in this part of the campaign is to raise both expendable and endowed funds to support key faculty retention and recruitment initiatives—research stipends, summer programs, materials, graduate support and course development, as well as endowed chairs and professorships. Each school and unit has its own push underway to boost faculty support in the campaign.

The College of Arts and Science's Spray-Randleigh Fellowship program is among the excellent examples of this impact. Funded by a $1.2 million expendable gift from the Spray Foundation of Atlanta and the Randleigh Foundation Trust of Chapel Hill, this program provides $15,000 summer supplements to new and current faculty members. Since 2002, 45 faculty fellows have benefited, including nine new recruits whose decisions to come to Carolina were clearly influenced by the fellowship offers.

Across the University, donors to Carolina First have created 127 endowed professorships toward our goal of 200. We have now filled 28 of those professorships, and the legislature just increased the state matching funds for distinguished endowed professorships. Overall, we have exceeded the $1.3 billion mark toward our campaign goal of $1.8 billion. We are very pleased with this progress.

Create Richest Learning Environment for Students

Our second priority is to create the richest possible learning environment for undergraduate, graduate, and professional students. One distinctive feature of Chapel Hill that sets us apart from the other great research universities is the culture for learning on this campus. It rivals that of the finest private liberal arts colleges for undergraduates, and the finest graduate and professional school environments for those students.

We are justifiably proud of that culture, but we must not be complacent about it. We must find ways to make it even better. Here are some concrete goals:

We should continue to increase the percentage of undergraduate classes with fewer than 20 students by doubling the size of the Honors Program. An endowment of $25 million would allow us to add 14 faculty positions to targeted departments in the College for this purpose. Let us focus on the six-year graduation rate, which currently stands at more than 82 percent. This is very good, but not good enough. Let us resolve to move this to at least 92 percent, the highest level of any of our public peers.

Our learning environment for graduate and professional students is closely linked with the vigor and excellence of our research enterprise. A key element of that, however, will be our ability to attract the finest graduate student talent. Thus, we must redouble our efforts to make graduate teaching assistant stipends nationally competitive. And we should seek to increase state funding for graduate tuition remission.

Invest in Centers of Research Excellence

Third, we must continue to invest in centers of research excellence. It is a marvelous tribute to the faculty that our research funding has risen steadily for more than two decades, solidifying Carolina's role as a top university.

This past year, faculty secured $577 million in research funds—up 7.5 percent from 2003, but shy of the double-digit increases we have seen for the past several years. Most observers expect increases in federal funding to slow even more. While that is surely a concern, I see it as an opportunity to turn to other sources.

For example, less than 2 percent of our funding comes from industry, compared to more than 20 percent at Duke and roughly 5 percent at most of our national public peers. There are, to be sure, legitimate concerns about industry-funded research: we must guard the integrity of our research, that it remains free and independent of inappropriate influence from any funding source. We can grow our industry-supported funding and remain faithful to our core principles.

The academic plan outlines areas of excellence and future opportunity for investment in five broad, interdisciplinary areas: biological, medical, and technology sciences; fine arts, humanities, and social sciences; global citizenship; social problem solving; and ethics, leadership, and public life. These are the academic areas in which Carolina is best positioned to make a difference. I could cite many examples, but let me pick just one.

Last year, we launched the Institute for Renaissance Computing, a new interdisciplinary partnership with Duke University, NC State, and the private sector in Research Triangle Park, under the leadership of Dan Reed. This institute offers enormous potential to catalyze research collaborations and economic development opportunities.

I have also asked Vice Chancellor Reed to lead a major strategic planning effort for information technology, encompassing everything from high-speed computing to what we know will be necessary major investments in administrative computing to replace systems that are increasingly obsolete. We have not fully tapped leading-edge information technology as an intellectual lever to help advance the University's mission. And we have not yet fully realized the potential of the Carolina Computing Initiative. This will be a major effort. The leading public university must lead in technology.

Enhance Global, Local Engagement

Our fourth priority is to enhance Carolina's engagement with North Carolina and the world. I have already shared my thoughts about sustaining our engagement with the state. However, I think engagement needs to be understood in global, as well as local, terms. The great universities of the 21st century will be defined by their presence on a worldwide stage. The quality of the educational experience, the significance of our research, will be judged by the extent to which it is truly global in nature.

We are building on existing strengths. We have study-abroad programs in nearly 70 different countries, and our students and faculty are engaged around the world through hundreds of academic programs, partnerships, and collaborations. Later this fall, we will break ground for the Global Education Center that will help bring our international efforts under one roof and serve as a vibrant hub of international teaching, research, and public service.

I include in this category of engagement our commitment to diversity, as an element of educational quality, since it is one way that we reflect the reality of the world and the state in which we live. Our students will be the poorer if we are not successful in creating a truly inclusive community.

I have appointed a Chancellor's Task Force on Diversity, chaired by Archie Ervin, to assess the state of diversity at Carolina and to produce a report this year to guide our vision for being a diverse campus. Our engagement with the state and the world will be incomplete, and we cannot be a leading university, if we do not model as a community the potential for people of diverse backgrounds and beliefs to live and work together within a framework of honor, integrity, compassion, and mutual respect.

Complete Development Plan; Start Carolina North

Fifth, we must successfully complete the campus development plan and begin Carolina North.[3] The first is critical because of the trust that the people of

North Carolina have placed in us through the passage of the higher education bond referendum. We have an enormous responsibility to see that this entire complex of projects, which is among the largest capital construction programs on any American campus, is successfully completed.

The initial implementation of Carolina North must be included in all our thinking. This project has issues and problems to be resolved before it can move forward, but we must keep focused on the ultimate goal and not relinquish the opportunity to leverage the research of this University directly into the state's economy.

Carolina North is our future, and it is vital to the state's economic success.

Strategic Investments Toward Highest Priorities

Sixth, we must determine strategies to acquire and allocate resources to our highest priorities. The Board of Trustees was strong in its determination that we really put our money where our mouth is—that we are clear and direct in acquiring and moving resources to support our highest priorities.

I affirm this wholeheartedly and like to point to one compelling example. In this past year, we successfully increased the percentage of classes with fewer than 20 students and reduced the percentage of classes with more than 50 students.

This is one of our measures of excellence, and it is one of the metrics used by *U.S. News and World Report*. This improvement helped us gain 21 places among all universities in their most recent assessment of faculty resources. In tough times, in the midst of budget cuts, we moved money, mainly in the College of Arts and Sciences, to support our priority.

Define Leadership Role

Finally, our seventh priority is to define Carolina's role as a leader. We take seriously our vision of being a leader within the state and within the UNC system. We are doing that with the Citizen-Soldier Initiative, funded by the U.S. Department of Defense. Our partners include faculty from NC State, UNC-Charlotte, East Carolina, Fayetteville State, and Duke Divinity School, along with UNC-TV and universities outside North Carolina.

A team of Carolina's faculty—led by Dennis Orthner in the School of Social Work, and Doug Robertson in the Highway Safety Research Center—helped conceive this national demonstration project. They have worked with our partners to create a program to support newly deployed and returning military reservists and National Guard soldiers and their families. This effort will bring employers, schools, child-care providers, health professionals, and faith-based organizations into a broad network of family support. Our response to these families shows the reach of a top-tier research university and its capacity to improve lives. It is a great example of a university that is leading.

I am visiting other UNC campuses as I travel this state. This fall, I met with Chancellor DePaolo in Wilmington, and we discussed potential academic partnerships. This is a role we should pursue more actively, finding ways to partner with our sister institutions, as well as with North Carolina's community colleges.

Conclusion

Two years ago, I introduced the concept of our being both good and great. Much of what I have focused on today has been about the goodness of the University, our commitment to engagement and public service and our core values as a public institution.

But let us not take our eye off the ball of excellence, on what it will take for us to become a truly distinguished world-class university—great as well as good. There are only four or five universities in this country that can even presume to have this conversation, to talk about being America's leading public university.

This is not so much a competition with other universities as it is with ourselves and with our own vision of excellence in harmony with our core values as a public university. Leaders of the University of Virginia speak publicly about privatizing the university. Certainly, Virginia's story is not our story. It is so radically different that my colleague, Law Dean Gene Nichol, has often said that if Thomas Jefferson were alive today, he would be a Tar Heel.

Our task is, as Judith Wegner put it recently, "to reimagine the public university for the 21st century and to stay focused on our core values, on our very soul as a public university." She is exactly right.

Substance over image, or in the words of our state's motto:

"Esse quam videri: to be rather than to seem."

Notes

1. Ashby, Warren. *Frank Porter Graham: A Southern Liberal.* Winston-Salem, N.C.: John F. Blair, Publisher, 1980, p. 151.

2. Nichol, Gene. "Ignoring Inequality." In: *Where We Stand: Voices of Southern Dissent.* Edited by Anthony Dunbar, Montgomery, Ala.: NewSouth Books, 2004, pp. 62–63.

3. Carolina North was envisioned as a mixed-use academic campus on university-owned property on Martin Luther King Jr. Boulevard, two miles north of the main campus. University and Town of Chapel Hill representatives signed a development agreement in 2009 that covers the first 20 years of development on the site. The agreement contains guidelines and standards for the development of the first 3 million square feet of a mixed-use research and academic campus on 133 acres. After the economic crash of 2009, the university put the development of Carolina North on hold.

2005 STATE OF THE UNIVERSITY ADDRESS

The University of North Carolina at Chapel Hill
September 15, 2005

*T*HE 2005 ADDRESS SEEKS *to balance two somewhat opposing thrusts— to be a global university, a player on the world stage, on the one hand, and to be a relevant presence for the people and policy makers of North Carolina, on the other. Over the summer, I had traveled to Asia and participated in the joint meeting of the Association of American Universities with the Association of Pacific Rim Universities. I also had extensive conversations with the leadership of Singapore National University, beginning a significant bi-lateral relationship with that institution.*

I felt it was essential to balance this emphasis on globalism with a demonstrated concern for our own state. I announced Carolina's participation in the new UNC Research Campus in Kannapolis, on the grounds of the old Pillowtex plant; a new Task Force on Engagement, a federally funded program to assist K–12 education across the state, a Task Force on Diversity, and—building on remarks of a year earlier—a firm commitment to move forward on Carolina North as the site for innovation. (In reflection, this is one of my major disappointments. We were never able to get across the starting line on this project.)

A Global University for North Carolina

Over the summer, my wife Susan and I led a delegation from Chapel Hill to Singapore and Bangkok. Our trip had several purposes, one of which was to participate in a meeting of university presidents and chancellors representing the Association of American Universities and our counterparts from the Association of Pacific Rim Universities who came from Australia, China, India, Japan, Thailand, and South America. We were hosted by the National University of Singapore, which was celebrating its centennial.

While in Singapore, we met 25 rising Carolina sophomores, several faculty members and alumni benefactors Alston Gardner and Barb Lee. We heard our students, many of whom were studying abroad for the first time, discuss their experiences. We also traveled to Bangkok to visit Kenan Institute Asia, which is playing a key role in Thailand's economic development.

Our colleagues at the National University of Singapore took advantage of their role as conference host, not only to celebrate their centennial, but also to announce their vision for a place on the global stage as a leading world university. The city state of Singapore has made a strategic decision to support NUS by investing heavily in its future. We heard from national leaders who made a compelling case for the power of higher education to shape a successful future for their country.

We explored additional relationships between Carolina and NUS, as well as other universities in Asia. UNC has extensive relationships with NUS, but several other American research universities have an even larger presence in Singapore than we do. Our delegation met with their provost and senior deans to discuss our existing programs as well as new ones, including a proposed undergraduate degree between the two universities. They also had this message for us: for years, they said, you American universities have been trolling in our waters for faculty and graduate students. Now we are going to troll in your waters.

Here is the lesson of these conversations: We are in a competition with this and other international universities, and our global partners are also our competitors. Singapore not only has an eye on the United States and Western Europe, but an even more acutely wary eye on their neighboring giants, China and India, both of which are making huge investments in their universities and in research. Singapore's former ambassador to the United Nations, Tommy Koh, in a speech to our conference, put the expansion of these two countries in stunning perspective, citing annual growth rates approaching 8 and 9 percent. "The rise of China and India are the two biggest growth stories of this century," Koh said. "If they succeed, they will inevitably change the world."[1]

Before leaving for Asia, I had just finished reading Thomas Friedman's *New York Times* best seller, *The World Is Flat: A Brief History of the Twenty-first Century*, and this book was fresh on my mind. Friedman's thesis is that the playing field of ideas and innovation—the fuel of a knowledge economy and once the province of the United States and the developed world—is wide open. Friedman draws from those who have called this new phenomenon the "globalization of innovation."[2] The job loss we are now experiencing to China and India is not just low-paying, semi-skilled manufacturing jobs, but high-paying, knowledge-based technology-sector jobs. The next wave could mean the potential loss of our international leadership in innovation and creativity.

In describing the rapidly changing environment of international competition, Friedman uses a metaphor that we should be quick to grasp at Carolina: basketball. Most of us can remember when the United States Olympic team was preeminent. We sent our best college athletes and won easily. But then the world took it up a notch, and we responded by sending in our pros. However, the 2004 American team, made up of NBA stars, lost to Puerto Rico, Lithuania, and Argentina and came home with a bronze. Previously, the United States had lost only one game in the history of the Olympics.

Next year in the City of Beijing alone, more students will take the SAT than in the entire United States. China has 1.3 billion people, and its government is making huge investments in its universities. Our country is on an opposite track. Federal funding for research in the physical and mathematical sciences and engineering, as a share of gross domestic product (GDP), declined by 37 percent between 1970 and 2004. When we should be doubling our investments in basic research, just to keep up with the rest of the world, we are making cuts.[3]

The key to retaining and creating jobs in this international competition is an educated, well-trained workforce. But consider these developments:

- The National Science Board reports the percentage of scientific papers written by Americans has fallen 10 percent since 1992.[4]
- By 2010, if current trends continue, over 90 percent of the world's scientists and engineers will live in Asia.[5]
- The United States is falling behind in producing college graduates, especially new Ph.D.'s in science and technology. North Carolina is in the lowest quartile of all 50 states for the production of Ph.D.'s in science and technology as a percentage of population.[6]

Our situation is particularly troubling if you look at the state of American science education at the pre-college level. Test results of fourth- and eighth-graders in science and math worldwide should be a wake-up call for all of us. For example, 44 percent of eighth-graders in Singapore scored at the most advanced level in math, as did 38 percent in Taiwan. Only 7 percent of American students scored at the most advanced level.[7]

Leadership That Matters for North Carolina

So, what does this mean for us? For UNC? For North Carolina?

First, North Carolina must compete in this global economy, so it is absolutely critical that its flagship university be a player on the world stage. We must be engaged internationally. Our new Global Education Center, now under construction, is a visible and tangible symbol of that commitment.

Second, we are called to deepen our engagement with North Carolina. Globalization strikes fear in many hearts across our state, which has been so heavily stricken with job loss. Peter Coclanis, associate provost for international affairs, describes this well in a paper that he read last year at our "Globalization and the American South" conference. Peter's paper, "Down Highway 52: Globalization, Higher Education, and the Economic Future of the American South," asks the question that I want to pose today: What is the role of a great university in a state that wants to be—indeed must be—fully competitive in a global economy?[8]

If there is one thing I have learned in my travels to nearly 50 communities last year around the state, it is this: our University is deeply engaged in the issues that matter most to North Carolinians—their health, their economy, and their education, both for themselves and their children. In every place I have visited, from the mountains to the coast, I have seen our students, faculty, and staff making a difference and touching people's lives.

Health Care

I have enjoyed stops at several of our Area Health Education Centers. AHEC is a shining example of an outreach program that improves the health of North Carolinians in every part of the state. We coordinate a sophisticated array of educational and clinical programs, increasing the supply of health-care providers and enhancing the quality of care to patients.

A key component of AHEC's service mission is Medical Air Operations, based at Horace Williams Airport. We plan to relocate Medical Air to Raleigh-Durham Airport when we begin the development of Carolina North. Last May, I pledged to keep Horace Williams Airport open until site work for Carolina North begins in approximately three years.

We are absolutely committed to both AHEC and Carolina North. We are not satisfied with maintaining the status quo when it comes to health care for our citizens. With shortages increasing for health professionals, we have bold plans for AHEC. We will seek support this year to expand our training capacity to meet the growing need for dentists, pharmacists, nurses, physicians, and other health-care professionals. We will look to AHEC for leadership in improving the diversity of the health-care workforce and addressing unacceptable disparities in health care.

Economic Development

The change in the economic landscape of North Carolina affects all its communities, and those dependent upon farming and manufacturing have been especially disrupted. But as I pointed out earlier, no sector of the economy, no sector of the state, is immune from global competition.

We have a great opportunity to reach out to one particularly hard-hit region through the initiative announced Monday in Kannapolis. The North Carolina Research Campus is a promising partnership with the Dole Food Company and the UNC System. We intend to leverage our own research strengths in obesity, nutrition, and disease prevention in the development of a new biotechnology and research campus on the site of the former Pillowtex plant.

This project could be yet another great example of how this University is reaching out beyond Chapel Hill and the Research Triangle.

Expanding our Capacity for Innovation

We fully intend to expand this University's capacity for innovation. The best example is Carolina North, our new campus for living and discovery, a place where we will engage in a significant way with the private sector and create affordable housing for faculty and staff in a beautiful environment that will allow people to live near their workplace. We presented the concept for Carolina North to the Board of Trustees in May. The trustees voted unanimously to authorize us to move ahead in working with our potential partners, as well as the towns of Chapel Hill and Carrboro.

An economic impact study estimates that Carolina North will generate 7,500 local jobs and about $48 million in annual tax revenues by the year 2020. More importantly, the study confirmed that Carolina North has the potential to position UNC as a leading national center for public–private partnerships. Carolina North will be a catalyst for the state's economic transformation.

The state's universities are the engine for the new economy for North Carolina. Our challenge is to maximize our capacity to help fuel that transformation.

Public Schools

A fundamental problem facing North Carolina is K–12 education. The numbers I cited earlier send a clear message that our public education system in North Carolina is not keeping pace with 21st-century needs.

We have several programs that reflect the University's growing involvement in K–12 education. For example, LEARN North Carolina is a collaborative statewide network of teachers and partners devoted to improving student performance and teacher proficiencies. Its Website in our School of Education receives 10,000 visitors per day and provides support to teachers and students in all North Carolina counties.

Destiny and Discovery, our traveling science laboratories, just received additional funding from the General Assembly. This program provides students with hands-on wet-lab science experience and critical classroom materials for teachers. I've watched children in several schools experience the innovative science available in these buses, and their enthusiasm is contagious.

Chancellor's Task Force on Engagement with North Carolina

Our overall contributions to the state and region are considerable. The Institute of Government, AHEC, and the Carolina Center for Public Service—these are all wonderful examples of how the University is engaged with the state. But I see two problems. First, as a University community, we are not organized for the best possible coordination of our outreach and engagement. Often the left hand does not know what the right hand is doing. People around the state are often uninformed about the actual involvement of this University in their communities, or where to go if they have a problem.

We can and must do more. We have a responsibility to continue leading and probing with humility and curiosity opportunities to match our resources with the state's needs. Our commitment to engagement and public service is part of Carolina's genetic code.

Therefore, I am convening a panel of University leaders to recommend how we might most effectively mobilize our resources. I am asking a number of senior officers to work directly with me as a special task force to address this question. These challenges facing our state are urgent, and we must respond accordingly.

Their recommendations should reflect an understanding of the work already underway, emphasize specific strategies to improve these efforts, respond to areas of unmet need, and identify resources to assure a continuity of effort. The task force will report preliminary findings and recommendations by the end of December.

A Special Focus on K–12 Education

There is one problem facing North Carolina that we cannot wait to engage—not even for the time it will take this task force to report—and that is the problem of our public schools. To live up to our calling to be the nation's leading public university, our light must shine with greatest intensity where it is most needed. Nothing calls us more urgently than the challenge of improving public schools in this state.

The U.S. Department of Education has awarded our School of Education a $10 million grant to be the nation's lead school of education tackling rural school reform. Through our National Research Center on Rural Education Support, our faculty will provide support to teachers and develop programs for students. We can make North Carolina the leading state in school reform.

However, that is only a start. Working under the umbrella of the engagement task force, I am asking the dean of our School of Education, Thomas James, to spearhead a bold initiative that will mobilize us to help the state's schools achieve dramatic gains in teaching and learning for all children. But this problem is not the province of the School of Education alone. I am committing Carolina's full range of intellectual power to address these complex issues.

Dean James will also work directly with State Board of Education Chair Howard Lee on this strategy for engagement with our public schools. At our summer retreat for deans and vice chancellors, Chairman Lee appealed to us to create a network of faculty, including but going beyond the School of

Education, who can respond to critical issues facing public school teachers, much as our Institute of Government faculty respond to the needs of public officials around the state. He also pointed to the critical need for leadership at the level of the local school. I will ask the engagement task force to study these proposals from Chairman Lee.

We have made great strides to ensure that UNC is accessible and affordable to low-income and middle-class students. The Carolina Covenant and its promise of a debt-free education to qualified needy students is widely recognized nationally. It has become a blueprint, not only for admitting deserving students from low-income families, but also for ensuring their academic success. I am pleased that our first class of scholars did exceptionally well. We had an attrition rate of 2.2 percent to the second year. To ensure the continued success of these students, we have launched a faculty mentoring program led by Fred Clark, associate dean of academic services. Let me recognize Fred and those faculty volunteers. I look forward to even more progress with this year's second class of 344 Covenant Scholars admitted under expanded eligibility requirements announced in last year's State of the University Address.

Diversity Task Force

Diversity is a key component of our academic plan. Last year, a special diversity task force underscored the importance of diversity on this campus.

We have made tremendous progress since the racial integration of the University 50 years ago, and from the days when women were not admitted.

We have seen improvement in the diversity of our full-time permanent faculty, especially among female African-Americans and male and female Asians and Hispanics. But we have made frankly little progress among African-American males.[9] We need to examine what is working and what is not. One of the programs that is clearly working is the Carolina Postdoctoral Program for Faculty Diversity. This state-supported program, begun in 1983, develops scholars from underrepresented groups for possible tenure-track appointments at UNC and other research universities. Twenty-one program graduates now hold tenure-track jobs at Carolina, and another 78 serve on faculties of other universities.

However, the essence of the diversity we seek is not something that can be captured in data. It is intangible; it deals with the spirit, with the culture of the campus.

I want to extend this idea to every dimension of human interaction, including race, religion, politics, and sexuality. Some of these categories are the very fault lines in the culture wars in America today. This is our raison d'être. This University was created at the beginning of the American republic to be a laboratory for democracy. We can show America how to have civil discourse about difficult topics.

We can have a campus culture where gays and lesbians feel welcome, where faith-based groups and political conservatives, as well as liberals, feel that their voice can be heard and respected, and we can do this without adopting speech codes or infringing upon the First Amendment or academic freedom. We can do this.

Archie Ervin, the associate provost for diversity and multicultural affairs, will lead the development of a diversity plan for Carolina, which can have a positive impact on every aspect of our life together on this campus.

Faculty Salaries and Campus-Based Tuition Increases

A great university starts and ends with a great faculty. Thus, the number one priority for this University remains attracting and retaining the finest faculty in the world.

As we benchmark ourselves against our national academic peers, we have worked hard to make up lost ground—to stay competitive with America's and the world's best universities.

Last year, faced with increasing competition from private universities, we again held steady with the overall faculty retention rate. From 32 external offers, we retained 21 faculty members and lost 11 to other institutions. The year before, we retained 43 faculty and lost 26, reversing a negative pattern from the year before that.

Our real success, however, has been the ability to reward faculty based on merit and achievement, not just responding to raids. A pre-emptive strategy of recognition and reward always trumps a reactive strategy of offers and counter-offers. No one should feel that recognition only comes through an external offer.

I am encouraged that the Board of Governors has launched a study of the competitive needs of research universities and has established a task force on tuition policy that includes our Trustee Chair Nelson Schwab. Meanwhile, our own Tuition Task Force has just begun its work this fall. No one likes tuition increases, and our request to the Tuition Task Force is to study carefully the needs of this campus and to ask only for that which is truly necessary to maintain the high quality of a Carolina education.

Last year, we raised money for 25 new endowed faculty chairs through the Carolina First Campaign. The General Assembly appropriated $8 million in recurring funds across the UNC System to match these gifts and doubled the amount to be matched by the state. Our share of these new state funds totaled $4.3 million, clearing the way for 18 of the 25 new chairs to be fully funded.

Staff Salaries and Benefits

Staff salaries and benefits remain a great concern. While we all appreciate this year's salary increase from the Legislature, I know that many of you just received notification from the State Health Plan about the sharp increase in your out-of-pocket costs. This is yet just another sign that the state's benefits package is increasingly non-competitive with the private sector and with peer institutions in other states.

We will continue looking for opportunities to take positive action when we can, particularly for employees at the bottom end of the pay scale. Effective last week, we increased annual salaries for all eligible full-time permanent staff to no less than $20,800. That exceeds by at least $688 the most recent action taken by the General Assembly. We have made these in-range adjustments, based on a market study, following state employee procedures and policies. Besides these salary increases, the University is making additional salary adjustments for other lowest-paid staff based on equity. In addition, Dr. Bill Roper, CEO of the UNC Health Care System, is implementing a similar plan for health-care system employees that will take effect early next month.

The work of our employees is important to our academic success. We operate in the highly competitive Research Triangle labor market, and we must compete to keep our very best employees.

Affordable Housing

One issue of concern for both faculty and staff is the need for affordable housing in Chapel Hill and Carrboro. I am pleased, therefore, to announce our intention to build new affordable housing for UNC faculty and staff on a portion of a 63-acre tract that we own close to Carolina North. Details are pending. We hope to create a neighborhood of approximately 140 single-family homes, town homes and condominiums. We are doing this to benefit our faculty and staff. It will be our first venture in building homes for faculty and staff to own, but it will not be our last. We will build even more in Carolina North.

Merit- and Need-Based Scholarships

Carolina attracts great students, and the best of these students have many opportunities. In the past, we have lost some to other universities offering merit-based scholarships. We intend to intensify our recruitment of students with exceptional academic and leadership potential, but we shall not do this at the expense of our support for need-based awards. Some institutions have actually diverted funds from need-based aid to recruit high-ability students. That approach is contrary to our values. Rather, we are building a merit-based scholarship program upon a strong foundation that takes care of need first. Few universities can declare, as we do, that they meet 100 percent of the demonstrated financial need of their students.

Last year, our trustees, responding to a creative proposal from Faculty Chair Judith Wegner, voted to allocate all the proceeds from the sale of trademark-licensed products to scholarships and financial aid. As a result, we created 55 new merit-based scholarships this year.

Through the Carolina First Campaign, we intend to raise $60 million to support additional merit-based scholarships. To jump-start this drive, I am delighted to announce a $10 million bequest from the estate of alumnus Colonel John Harvey Robinson. Within one year of investment, we expect this fund will provide $500,000 annually for new merit-based scholarships. Colonel Robinson's generosity will assist us in attracting the best and the brightest to Chapel Hill.

We will also work to increase the support for need-based awards. We have had great success in seeking support for the Carolina Covenant, for which we have raised almost $3.5 million. We shall continue to seek additional support for this great program with the goal of a $10 million endowment.

Master Plan Update

Last fall, we began updating our campus master plan. We remain committed to the bedrock principles of this plan. The bottom line is we are fast approaching the full build-out of the main campus, thanks to a pace of construction that greatly exceeds that envisioned in the original plan. Completion of the main campus and Carolina North together are the future of the University.

As part of our efforts to engage the campus and larger community in this work, we are scheduling additional briefings for the community and the Chapel Hill Town Council. After briefing the council on the master plan update, we will then seek town approval for modifications to our current development plan. At the same time, we will begin conversations with our neighbors in Chapel Hill and Carrboro, as well as with the regional and state transportation and traffic authorities, about key issues related to Carolina North, including transportation and traffic, fiscal equity, and environmental issues.

A Renaissance of the Arts

We have made enormous strides in science and technology over the past five years. I am enormously proud of what we have accomplished in adding people, equipment, and facilities in areas including genomics, advanced materials science, nanotechnology, biotechnology, bioinformatics, and information technology, among others. We will continue to pursue excellence in these areas.

But being a great university also includes strength in the arts and humanities. Last weekend, the University community enjoyed the re-opening of Memorial Hall, which, I truly believe, marks the beginning of a renaissance for the arts at Carolina. For me, this is a long-awaited reality. I believe in the power of the arts to transform the human spirit. We don't talk much about the spirit in this secular university, but we should. The arts can provide the platform for the deepest expressions of what it means to be human. The restoration of Memorial Hall and the new Carolina Performing Arts Series is only the beginning. We also want to enhance the bonds between our academic units in art, dramatic art, and music, as well as with existing organizations such as the PlayMakers Repertory Company. Ultimately, the realization of the arts common, including the restoration of Old Playmakers Theatre, Gerrard Hall, the expansion of the Ackland Art Museum, and a new music building, will constitute the full story.

The essence of this renaissance, however, is not in buildings, but in people and programs, representing a tangible bridge to the communities beyond the campus. We invested in this first year of the Carolina Performing Arts program to launch this new series at a level commensurate with a great university, but we cannot sustain it with University funds alone. We have set a goal of a $10 million endowment to continue this high level of program activity. I am delighted to announce a challenge grant of $5 million from the William R. Kenan, Jr. Charitable Trust to help us realize this goal.

Let me also challenge our faculty to find ways to integrate the arts into their teaching, and challenge our students to take advantage of the $10 tickets that are available to them for each one of the 40-plus performances in Memorial Hall. My hope for Carolina is that these presentations, plus the countless other student performances and public lectures that will take place in this wonderfully restored hall, will invigorate the intellectual life of this University, restoring that richness and fabric that we have so missed these past three years.

Ars longa vita brevis.

Hail to the brightest star of all. Carolina.

Notes

1. Koh, Tommy. "Three Messages for America From an Asian Who Loves America." Remarks delivered July 1, 2005, in Singapore to the Association of American Universities – Association of Pacific Rim Universities Presidents Roundtable, p. 2.

2. Friedman, Thomas L. *The World is Flat: A Brief History of the Twenty-First Century*. New York, N.Y.: Farrar, Straus and Giroux, 2005, p. 30.

3. Friedman, p. 268.

4. Friedman, p. 269.

5. *Tapping America's Potential: The Education for Innovation Initiative*. Published by The Business Roundtable, July 2005, p. 1. (http://www.businessroundtable.org/pdf/20050803001TAPfinalnb.pdf)

6. *Science and Engineering Indicators 2004*. Published by the National Science Board, National Science Foundation, Division of Science Resources Statistics, Arlington, Va., May 2004, Table 8-8. (http://www.nsf.gov/sbe/srs/seind04/)

7. Friedman, pp. 271–272.

8. Coclanis, Peter A. "Down Highway 52: Globalization, Higher Education, and the Economic Future of the American South." *The Journal of the Historical Society*, Fall 2005, Vol. 5, pp. 331–345.

9. *Report of the Chancellor's Task Force on Diversity*, April 26, 2005, pp. 12–14. (http://www.unc.edu/minorityaffairs/assessment/diversityreport.pdf)

2006 STATE OF THE UNIVERSITY ADDRESS

The University of Chapel Hill
September 12, 2006

THE THEME OF THIS *address might be "Good to Great; Good and Great," building on the themes of best-selling author Jim Collins. These are not new themes, but they are sounded more strongly here than previously. Also notable is an almost muscular sense of momentum and accomplishment.*

This address sets some ambitious goals—what Collins calls "big, hairy, audacious goals," the biggest being the goal of reaching $1 billion in external research funding by 2015. Tony Waldrop, the Vice Chancellor for Research, advised me that this goal, while a stretch, was attainable. UNC announced it had reached $1 billion in research funding in 2015. As Napoleon is said to have remarked, the quality he most sought in his generals was good luck. I also set ambitious goals for faculty retention and student graduation rates.

More than anything else, this speech celebrates excellence. It concludes with the idea of good and great—a celebration of an excellent university with core values. "Excellence with a heart," was my definition of "The Carolina Way."

OVER THE PAST SEVERAL years, we have talked about what it means to be a great university—to be the leading public university in America—striving for greatness.

Jim Collins, author of the best-selling book *Good to Great*, defines greatness not as a function of circumstance. Greatness, he says, "is largely a matter of conscious choice."

Collins describes Carolina's approach. We have made tough decisions and instilled discipline in our budget. Our priorities mark the way. We are driven to be better.

Like Collins, we have a conviction that greatness is a journey, not a destination. The moment we think of ourselves as great, he says, we will have begun our slide into mediocrity.

We have also talked about being good—good in the context of maintaining high ethical and moral values—goodness as critical to achieving greatness.

The single most distinguishing feature of this University is its goodness—its core values of commitment to the people of North Carolina and the betterment of humankind. Charles Kuralt nailed it in his 1993 Bicentennial remarks when he said:

"Here we found something in the air. A kind of generosity, a certain tolerance, a disposition toward freedom of action and inquiry that has made of Chapel Hill, for thousands of us, a moral center of the world."

So this is my thesis: we can aspire to greatness . . . move from good to great . . . and be both great and good.

The Quest for Excellence: Good to Great
Strengthening Faculty Recruitment and Retention

In our quest for greatness, our top priority remains unchanged—to continue to strengthen support for faculty—so we can recruit and retain the very best, and provide the tools faculty need to excel. This is the key to everything. It all starts with the faculty, and it quickly expands to staff and students.

We have an extraordinary academic culture—a true culture of excellence—and it is the magnet that attracts and keeps great faculty and staff. How many times have I heard our faculty say that their greatest joy is their colleagues—the pride of being associated with distinguished people in a collegial environment?

Let me share one example. Our chemistry department is recognized among the nation's best, and if forced to list our top five departments, I would include chemistry. This faculty has maintained its faith in each other and the University for years in the grossly inadequate Venable Hall, yet they consistently rank among our top-funded science departments. Now they are moving into their fabulous new building, the Lowry and Susan Caudill Laboratories.

Holden Thorp, chemistry's chair, says the core purpose of his department is creating new knowledge and producing confident, independent scientists. It is not and never has been about funding.

This is a department where colleagues celebrate one another's success, as they did the other day when one of them learned about a prestigious national award now pending the funding agency's formal announcement. This award will go to a valued colleague whom the department supported during some lean times, an outstanding teacher and advisor, as well as researcher. Chemistry gets it. It is going from good to great. It is just one example among many that I could cite at Carolina.

Another measure of the faculty's reputation is its presence in the national academies. Our two newest academy members are Christopher Browning, Frank Porter Graham Distinguished Professor of History, and Ted Salmon, the James Larkin and Iona Mae Ballou Distinguished Professor of Cell Biology. Professor Browning specializes in the history of the Holocaust and Nazi Germany. Professor Salmon studies the structures inside cells that play a role in how cells divide.

Last spring, they were selected to the American Academy of Arts and Sciences for preeminent contributions to their disciplines and society at large. The University now has 30 members in this academy, a mark of great prestige.

Professors Browning and Salmon both hold endowed professorships. Last year we created 29 new endowed professorships with gifts to the Carolina First Campaign, which had another record year in fiscal 2006. That brings us to 181 new professorships toward our goal of 200.

Of course, the most obvious and tangible elements in attracting and retaining great faculty are salaries and benefits. Thanks to this new state budget, supplemented with our own campus- and school-based tuition, we made great progress on faculty salaries. However, achieving our goals long term will require a sustained effort. Our Five-Year Financial Plan calls for reaching the 67th percentile for faculty salaries among our public and private peers by 2011. That will require average annual six percent legislative salary increases over the next five years, supplemented by modest campus-based tuition increases.

If the state makes this commitment, we can hold tuition increases to moderate and predictable levels. Until this most recent year, however, campus-based tuition has been our salvation in maintaining a competitive position for faculty.

Carolina's Distinctive Culture

When people ask what is distinctive about Carolina, I have a ready answer. It is the almost perfect balance we maintain between great research and a great learning environment for our students.

I see countless examples of our most respected, our most distinguished scholars excelling in the classroom—taking pride in the accomplishments of their students, engaging them in research and creativity. Such dedication among the faculty has been vital in the many successes we celebrate.

One of many examples is from the Department of Physics and Astronomy. Assistant Professor Daniel Reichart and his students documented the oldest known explosion—the afterglow of a gamma ray burst 12.8 billion years ago. Undergraduate Josh Haislip was the first to analyze that data from UNC's telescope in Chile, and Josh is the first author on the scholarly publication about this great discovery. That in itself is a tribute to Dr. Reichart and our academic culture.

This fall, we are implementing a new undergraduate curriculum, a once-in-a-generation event. The key word in this curriculum is *connections*—enhancing connections between classes, between disciplines, and between teaching and research.

Tied to the new curriculum is the Quality Enhancement Plan (QEP) developed as part of our 10-year reaccreditation. The QEP makes the student learning experience global and enhances undergraduate research. We have committed nearly $2.5 million over the next three years to implement the QEP, which together with the new curriculum combine to make a good university greater.

Recognizing the importance of graduate students, we have increased the minimum stipends for teaching assistants to $7,000 per semester, up $1,000 over last year and supported by campus-based tuition. The biggest advocates of this increase were our undergraduates, who know the importance of TAs. They know that this will help us recruit the very best graduate students to Chapel Hill.

We are the national leader for accessibility. *U.S. News and World Report* just ranked us first among public universities for the second consecutive year under the heading "Great Schools, Great Prices." *Kiplinger's Personal Finance Magazine* rated UNC as the best value among all publics for the fifth time.

To attract more high-achieving students, we have expanded merit-based scholarships. Through the Carolina First Campaign, we have created more than 600 scholarships and fellowships to support need and merit, a 60 percent increase since the campaign began. We now direct all our trademark licensing revenue to scholarships, allowing us to add 60 new merit scholarships last year, a number that increased to 68 scholarships this fall. Every time you buy a Carolina t-shirt, you are supporting scholarships.

Last year our students had tremendous success in winning distinguished national and international scholarships or fellowships. We led public universities with eight. Our students won a Rhodes, a Goldwater, two Luces, a Marshall, a Truman, and a Udall, as well as a spot on the USA Today All College Academic Team.

Improving Graduation Rates

With all this success, we can still be better. Graduation rates constitute one of the most important metrics in measuring undergraduate quality. I first raised this issue two years ago. Since then, the trustees have asked for a comprehensive plan this fall for improving graduation rates. President Bowles is asking every campus in the system to do this.

Currently, our graduation rates are 71 percent for four years and 84 percent for six years. These are the highest in the UNC system and above most of the Association of American Universities.

Our four-year rates exceed those for three of our most distinguished peers: Berkeley, UCLA, and Michigan. But our six-year rates lag behind this group by three percent. I shall propose to the trustees in November that we set a goal of matching the six-year graduation rates of these three universities—87 percent—and extending our four-year graduation rate to 75 percent by 2010.

We need to set an expectation for students to graduate in eight semesters, or four years. The faculty has approved measures to move us toward this goal. The new curriculum will strengthen and integrate our academic offerings. Next fall, students will be subject to new progress-toward-degree requirements and increased academic eligibility standards. To stay on track, students having difficulties will receive earlier warnings and more help from the University, including additional advisors. We want students to be ready to graduate on time as they begin the fourth year.

We should never be content with the status quo. Good enough is never good enough—not for an institution that aspires to be America's leading public university. Going from good to great.

Investing in Research Excellence: Fostering Success in Research and Creativity

Over the past six years, we have followed a strategy of investing in research centers of excellence. We have built nationally recognized programs in genomics and genetics, advanced materials science, and nanotechnology. Our scientists are making discoveries that will improve people's lives. Such work complements our great strengths in the social sciences, humanities, and the arts.

Our strategy has paid off. External funding was up nearly 2.4 percent, to $593 million from $579 million. While funding per se is not our goal, because it is competitive and peer-reviewed, it is our single best metric to evaluate our comparative position as a research university. One noteworthy success is the National Institutes of Health "Roadmap for Medical Research" initiatives. For the second year since the inception of the program, we led the nation with the most grants, this year with eight, ahead of Vanderbilt, Columbia, Memorial Sloan-Kettering Cancer Center, Johns Hopkins, Harvard, Stanford, and Duke.

This is very good, but we can do more. Let us today set a goal of securing $1 billion in external research funding by 2015. This is a challenge that the faculty and our campus community can and should embrace. It will not be easy, but we can do it.

This will require a significant investment by the State of North Carolina that is reflected in our budget request to President Bowles and General Administration. We can show the state an incredible return on the investment it already makes in faculty research. For example, the 11 centers and institutes reporting to the vice chancellor for research and economic development received more than $6 million in state funding for research in 2004–05 and brought in another $82 million in external grants and contracts. That represents a leveraging of almost $13 for every $1 of state support. The medical school's centers and institutes produce a return approaching $30 for every dollar in state support for research.

To realize our long-term goal, we must increase our computational capacity to support the faculty's interdisciplinary work, to be competitive for grants on a much larger scale. The Renaissance Computing Institute, or RENCI, is one critical lever that will make us more competitive with the National Science Foundation, the NIH, and other sources. When our plans are fully realized, RENCI will support initiatives that build upon existing strengths and help attract new talent. Achieving success will maintain our leadership position among research universities and generate economic benefits for North Carolina.

Let us be crystal clear about this: $1 billion is a stretch goal, more than $200 million above what we might be expected to reach at our current trajectory. Some have argued that this is too high . . . unrealistic . . . that the uncompensated cost of this research will be unaffordable. To use a Jim Collins term, this is a "big, hairy, audacious goal," appropriate for a university aspiring to be the leading public university. We should dream no small dreams.

At the same time, we must also remember to keep our balance, to maintain our strengths in the humanities and the arts, and to stay true to our commitment to great teaching. We do this now. We can do this with a stretch goal. Good to great. Great and good.

Becoming a Truly Global University

If there is a theme for this academic year, it is globalization. In the spring, we will dedicate the Global Education Center, which will bring together a robust array of academic programs, research, and student services. A major gift from the FedEx Corporation made possible the completion of the building.

Throughout 2007, the University will celebrate our accomplishments in global education. Next spring, we will dedicate our new European Study Center in London. This center will be a base for the Honors Program, augmenting a relationship with King's College, London.

Collaborations are flourishing with the National University of Singapore, where we have developed a joint undergraduate degree program that is pathbreaking among our U.S. peers. In last year's address, I recounted my visit with 25 of our students in Singapore. A few days ago, one of these students shared with his organ instructor, my wife Susan, his own excitement in showing our campus to students now here from Singapore.

We have more than 120 faculty and staff in working groups with China. We have signed several memorandums of understanding with collaborators and held joint programs with the Chinese government and Tsinghua University.

For the third consecutive year, we led all public research universities for the percentage of undergraduates studying abroad, nearly 37 percent. In 2000, our rate was about 15 percent. Six years ago in this address, I announced the goal that every undergraduate would have a significant international experience. These gains show that when we establish goals and pay attention to them, we can make good things happen, even great things.

Study abroad has increasingly become an integral part of the Carolina experience. Former Trustee Chair Earl "Phil" Phillips believes in the educational value of exploring other countries. He has established the Phillips Ambassadors Program with a generous gift that will provide scholarships to 50 undergraduates studying in Asia. This is a great example of enlightened philanthropy by our former U.S. Ambassador to the Eastern Caribbean.

Expanding Our Worldwide Reach in Health

Carolina is an international powerhouse in global health, with a significant presence around the world. In Malawi, our researchers are fighting to conquer infectious diseases, such as malaria and HIV/AIDS. In China and Madagascar, our scientists are helping stop the resurgence of syphilis. In 60 villages in India, we are working to improve the development of toddlers. We are active in South Africa, in Russia, Thailand, Cambodia, the Dominican Republic, South America, and the Caribbean.

Last year, we established a Partnership Program in Global Health, funded by the NIH with a $400,000 grant that the University is matching to expand our global health curriculum and research. Only 12 grants were awarded worldwide.

The Bill and Melinda Gates Foundation recognized our work with a $22 million grant for a clinical trial of a new oral drug to treat African sleeping sickness, which threatens the lives of millions. Our faculty led an international consortium in developing this drug. If approved, it would be the first new treatment for sleeping sickness in 50 years.

We will draw from the leadership of key faculty in medicine and public health to develop the UNC Institute for Global Health and Infectious Diseases. We are in the early stages of development, identifying funding and involving private partners and other institutions. It matters that our faculty bring such a sophisticated level of expertise to the world's health needs. This is what a great public research university does. It enables outstanding scientists to follow their commitment to discovery to help relieve human suffering and improve lives.

From Chapel Hill to the world. From good to great.

Strengthening the Culture

President Bowles has set in motion a process to make the entire UNC system more efficient and more effective, a process we will apply to some of our most critical issues.

Chief among them is replacing our aging information systems and re-engineering our business processes. This is no easy task. It is complicated by our antique technological infrastructure, our decentralized business processes, and a maze of federal and state regulations that must be accommodated. The result is a barely functioning complex of business services.

This as a huge challenge ... and an opportunity. I have asked Provost Gray-Little to head this project, working closely with Dan Reed and David Perry. Solving our technology problems will be a vast and expensive undertaking, affecting every aspect of the University. It begins by looking at all our business processes and asking the questions, "How many steps in this process are really necessary, and how many can we eliminate?"

The challenge, given our decentralization, will be for some of us to relinquish a process that we "own." We simply cannot hold ourselves above the need to change and adapt. We need to lead with innovation. The payoff will be a leaner, more nimble university. How important is this? I believe it is as critical to our future as our enormous capital construction program. If we do it well, it will be one of the ways we become the leading public university.

Leading with innovation. Going from good to great.

A University With a Strong Moral Center: Great and Good

I turn now to the second part of my thesis, the noble idea that Carolina can be both great and good—in Kuralt's words "a moral center of the universe," a great public university committed to access and affordability, to service and engagement, and to the conviction that our mission includes the development of the heart, as well as the mind.

Each year, we confer upon a select group of faculty and staff the C. Knox Massey Distinguished Service Award, which recognizes the incredible, selfless devotion of selected honorees. Let me take this opportunity to recognize this year's winners.

- Fred Clark, associate dean of academic services and professor of Romance languages. Fred is a true champion of our efforts to encourage student success through his work organizing mentors for the Carolina Covenant program.
- Ray Hackney, biological safety officer and industrial hygiene manager. Ray decodes complex federal and state regulations. When the Occupational Safety and Health Administration extended its rules to laboratories, one colleague wrote, "he saved us all."
- Larry Keith, assistant dean of medical school admissions and director of special programs. Larry has played a key role in the medical school's high graduation rates among African American and Native American students.
- Esther Ko, housekeeper. More than 20 students and others from Alexander Residence Hall nominated Esther because she goes above and beyond her job duties. One student called her "the embodiment of the Carolina Way."
- Don Luse, director of the Carolina Union. Don pushed to promote a "living room" atmosphere during the Union's renovations. He sees the importance of an environment that fosters intellectual and personal growth.
- Lynn Williford, assistant provost for institutional research and assessment. Her research skills are without compare, and they inform every key decision we make. Her work was a key component of our recent reaccreditation.

These are our very best colleagues.

This fall, we will move forward to launch a diversity plan drawn from the recommendations of the Task Force on Diversity. This plan sets five goals to advance our vision for a diverse and inclusive campus community. It emphasizes accountability, education, and further research, and I am grateful for the leadership of Associate Provost Archie Ervin.

Perhaps nothing embodies the spirit of the Carolina culture as well as the Carolina Covenant. The concept we developed has spread quickly to a growing list of public and private institutions. Next week we will host a national conference, "The Politics of Inclusion: Higher Education at a Crossroads."

This conference will examine the issue of access, with the clear intent to influence national policy and practice. This is the kind of event a leading university should convene.

Last year, we opened a new avenue of access from our neighboring community colleges when the Jack Kent Cooke Foundation selected Carolina to participate in a national program that will help community college students earn UNC degrees after completing two years in the community college. Students from Alamance, Durham, and Wake county community colleges will benefit directly from this program.

Engaging—With North Carolina and the World

One mark of our success with engagement is the health of our collaborations with our sister UNC system campuses. Last year, I traveled to several of them to explore new relationships. We have had conversations with colleagues at Western Carolina about a partnership involving basic research in Chapel Hill and applications technology in Cullowhee. RENCI is working with faculty at East Carolina, Appalachian State, and UNC-Asheville. Our School of Dentistry is partnering with East Carolina to help expand dentistry education there and, subject to the approval of the Board of Governors, to help create a new dentistry school in Greenville. Our marine sciences faculty here and in Morehead City have close working relationships with colleagues at UNC-Wilmington, ECU, and NC State. Our School of Pharmacy has established a strong collaboration with Elizabeth City State to deliver the Pharm.D. degree to northeastern North Carolina. And we have a long history of collaboration with NC State in biomedical engineering and in many other areas.

At the same time, we have been examining our own public service efforts. Last fall, I appointed the Engagement Task Force to recommend how we could intensify our service to North Carolina, especially in the areas of K–12 education, health, and economic development.

In education, our top priority is increasing the number of K–12 science and math teachers. This will require much closer collaborations between the School of Education and the College of Arts and Sciences, and our strategy will be to attract science and math majors into a fourth-year accelerated teaching major.

In health care, our number one strategy is to expand the professional workforce available to citizens. We will support enrollment increases in dentistry, medicine, nursing, pharmacy, public health, and social work. Related efforts include increasing access for students from economically distressed areas through a scholarship program.

In economic development, we envision a management academy for fledgling high-growth companies and a program to help state and local leaders build sustainable economies. Success will depend on how well our professional schools and social sciences departments join together to support communities that most need our help.

The task force also examined the question of the recognition and reward of engaged scholarship as a component of promotion, tenure, and merit salary evaluations. This will be an important conversation for us to have with the faculty.

Seizing Our Future: Carolina North

Our engagement with the state will be greatly enhanced by Carolina North, our 21st-century living-and-learning community.

We will pursue this project tirelessly because it is absolutely critical to our future. We want this new campus to be a national model for sustainability, addressing the long-term needs of the University for accelerated transfer of our new knowledge into the economy, housing for faculty and staff, and new collaborations with the private sector.

A Leadership Advisory Committee of community, state, and University representatives is recommending guiding principles for building Carolina North. Last month, I appointed Professor Jack Evans as executive director of Carolina North. Our trustees have directed us to submit our zoning and development plan applications to local governments by October 1st of next year.

We want the Carolina North campus to have an aesthetic quality that will draw people to it and enhance the communities surrounding it, just as the main campus has for two centuries.

We believe it can do all of that while at the same time advancing our missions of teaching, research, and public service.

Good to great.

Conclusion

Last June officially marked the 250th anniversary of the birth of William R. Davie, the University's founder and the creator of public higher education in America. Davie had a great vision for this University, created at the end of the 18th century and the beginning of the American era.

Today, we are the stewards of that great venture at the dawn of a new century and a world as new and daunting as the one Davie faced. We are called upon to make this University even greater—to go from good to great. We are also called on to nurture and nourish what it means to be a public university, to be both great and good. And we must adapt this great and noble institution to the 21st century.

Good to great.

Great and good.

2007 STATE OF THE UNIVERSITY ADDRESS

The University of North Carolina at Chapel Hill
September 26, 2007

IN THIS, MY LAST *address, I announced my intention to relinquish the position of Chancellor at the end of the academic year. There is an old saying that "timing is everything," and in many ways, my timing at Carolina was ideal, arriving in 2000 just before the voters approved the NC Higher Education Construction Bond, and ending my career in 2008, following the best legislative season in many years and just before the economic crash that occurred later in 2008. I was very fortunate.*

There was much to celebrate. All of the vital signs were positive. Carolina had made a national mark with the Carolina Covenant, widely recognized as the gold standard for need-based aid. Graduation rates, a critical mark of excellence, were trending up, and we were about to pass Berkeley and UCLA, which we did a year later. With the help of campus-based tuition increases as well as appropriations from the General Assembly, we were making real progress with faculty salaries. Retention rates for faculty were up. External research funding continued to trend up.

The Carolina First Campaign,[1] almost completed, was a stunning success. As of September, we had raised over $2 billion, and the total would reach $2.38 billion by the end of the campaign. The campus had undergone a physical transformation—$2.1 billion in new construction and renovation—not just more buildings, but a significantly more beautiful campus. I loved to point out *that we had taken twenty acres of asphalt and created ten new acres of green space while adding over 5 million new usable square feet. This was accomplished by major investments in free mass transit, park-and-ride, and parking structures.*

Carolina North seemed finally achievable in 2007, with an Innovation Center, constructed in partnership with a private developer, as a real possibility. This project crashed, and with it, any prospects for development on this site. (AHEC moved its air operations to Raleigh-Durham Airport, but Horace Williams Airport remained open for private aviation through 2017.) The University seems to have abandoned any immediate plans for Carolina North. The failure to realize this dream is my biggest disappointment as Chancellor.

With the state's economy humming, Carolina was under considerable pressure from the UNC system and the General Assembly to grow its enrollment. Controlling growth was my concern, lest we lose quality. When the economy crashed a year later, this pressure evaporated. My successor had other problems to deal with, but not this one.

GOOD AFTERNOON. LET US begin by recognizing several people who are important to the success of our university. We are honored to be joined by the President of the University of North Carolina, Erskine Bowles, and four former chancellors: William (Bill) Aycock, Christopher Fordham, Paul Hardin, and William O. McCoy. These are great leaders for North Carolina.

We also celebrate this year's winners of the C. Knox Massey Award for Distinguished Service. They are Terry Bowers, electronics technician; Carolyn Cannon, associate dean and academic advising director; Sue Klapper, now retired senior associate undergraduate admissions director; Michael O'Malley, associate director of the Lineberger Comprehensive Cancer Center; Kirk Pelland, director of the Grounds Services Department; and Wanda Thompson, a housekeeper in Winston Residence Hall. Each of these Tar Heels exemplifies great service.

State Budget Positions Carolina for Success

Let me say a word about the North Carolina General Assembly's budget, which may be the best in the University's history. I think the major reason for this success is President Bowles' dynamic leadership. Erskine, on behalf of all of us and the people of North Carolina, thank you. When Erskine came almost two years ago, he said he wanted to be our partner. He has been that and more. He is a leader we are proud to follow.

The General Assembly made a stunning series of allocations including meaningful salary increases for faculty, a well-deserved raise for our staff and the creation of the University Cancer Research Fund that will help put Chapel Hill on the map as one of the world's preeminent institutions leading cancer research. Other highlights included significant recurring funds to support excellence in the School of Law, capital construction for genomics and dentistry, and new faculty positions for the nutrition institute at the Kannapolis research campus.

Governor Easley and our legislative leaders—especially Senate President Pro Tem Marc Basnight and House Speaker Joe Hackney—demonstrated a keen recognition of the role that the UNC system is playing in North Carolina's future success. We are grateful.

Personal Comments

Before getting to the substance of today's remarks, please allow me some personal comments. People often ask if I dread making speeches, especially this big one every year. I have a confession. This is one of the most enjoyable aspects of my job.

Remember, I am a performing artist by profession. Performing can be a humbling experience. Early in my career I was about to give the final concert of a small Midwestern town's community artist series. Just before I went on, I heard the series board chair appeal to the audience to give generously to the series, in her words, "so that next year we can afford better artists."

The principal lesson I learned as a concert artist was always to get off the stage before the applause stopped. Nothing is more embarrassing than being stuck out there with no applause. The second lesson was to be conservative with encores. "Always leave them wanting more," my teachers said.

Those lessons stuck, and I think they apply to me as much today as they did in my years on the concert stage. Thus, I am announcing today that I shall relinquish the position of chancellor of this great University at the end of the fiscal year, June 30, 2008.

Let me hasten to add that this is not a retirement for me. After a year's research leave, I shall return to the campus with the most exalted title this

University can confer on an individual—*professor*. I make this announcement today to give the Board of Trustees time to begin a search for my successor, with the hope that this individual can assume his or her responsibilities on July 1, 2008.

I will be fully engaged as your chancellor in the year ahead. I know what I have told our fourth-year students will be equally true for me—that this year will pass in a flash, and before we know it, we will be in Kenan Stadium in graduation gowns. I do not intend to waste a minute.

Celebrating Success: Building Momentum for Excellence

This University is on an incredible roll. It is a great tribute to our students, faculty, staff, trustees, alumni, parents, and friends, as well as President Bowles and the leaders of the UNC system and North Carolina. There is a lot to celebrate in Chapel Hill, because we are making great progress on virtually every priority that we have set for ourselves.

Enhancing the Learning Environment

This year's first-year class is again the most academically qualified in Carolina's history. We received over 20,000 applications, up from 16,000 a decade ago. The average SAT score for this fall's first-year class was 1302; 10 years ago, it was 1220. This year 77 percent of our newest students graduated in the top 10 percent of their high school class; a decade ago it was 66 percent. This year's class is also more diverse than ever.[2]

Carolina leads the nation in access and affordability. Through several key policy decisions, Carolina has become more affordable to a larger number of North Carolinians than ever before. *Kiplinger's Personal Finance Magazine* has concluded six consecutive times that we are the best academic value in public higher education. Universities and entire states are following our lead when they model programs after the Carolina Covenant, and this May we will graduate our first class of Carolina Covenant Scholars.

We also set the bar high for graduation rates, a critical measure of undergraduate quality. Our goal is to match the six-year rates for Berkeley, UCLA, and Michigan by 2010. Last year, they were at 87 percent, while we were at 84 percent. It is too early to report progress on this front. On the four-year rate, even though last year's results exceeded those three same peers, we set a target of 75 percent by 2010. Here, I am pleased to report some success. Since last year, we have improved the four-year rate from 71 percent to 73 percent.

For the first time in several years, the General Assembly included additional funding for tuition remissions to help us recruit and retain outstanding graduate students, who constitute nearly 40 percent of our students. They are the faculty's partners in teaching and research and make invaluable contributions to undergraduate education.

Strengthening Faculty Resources

With regard to faculty, we have improved how we pay, recruit, and retain them because they are this University's number one priority. Our goal is to take average faculty salaries up to the 80th percentile of our peers. We are roughly at the 50th percentile, and we may reach the 80th percentile as early as next year with another solid legislative session and a modest increase in campus-based tuition.[3] State appropriations helped slash the gap between current salaries and the 80th percentile from about $21 million last year to $11 million this year for all tenure and tenure-track faculty. This is real progress.

More competitive salaries are helping recruitment and retention. Last year we retained 72 percent of faculty who received outside offers to whom we made counter offers. That was our best showing in five years. We were at 52 percent in 2006 and 40 percent in 2003. We received almost $1 million from the recruitment and retention fund created by the legislature at President Bowles' request. Those dollars helped attract nine nationally known scholars and keep six of our strongest faculty who received outside offers. Most importantly, as our salaries become more competitive, fewer faculty will even be tempted by outside offers. This is a healthier culture for all.

Nurturing Research and Creativity

This year faculty again demonstrated remarkable creativity in the advancement of new knowledge. The most critical problems of our society require all the resources of a great research university—in ethics and values, the creative arts, as well as science and technology. For example, cancer research is not just a medical or public health problem, nor is the study of the environment. This is where Carolina excels, where the low stone walls of our campus become a metaphor for our ability to work together to solve big problems.

For our science faculty, the principal metric of success is sponsored research. Total grants and contracts grew by 2.9 percent in 2007 to over

$610 million—more than double where we were a decade ago. These gains came even as funding from the National Institutes of Health began to shrink after its budget doubled in the 1990s. Our strategy of investing in big ideas, pulling together our strongest programs across the campus, has worked. This approach has paid big dividends in genomics, advanced material science, and nanotechnology. It has also worked in medieval and early modern studies, which just received a major grant from the Andrew J. Mellon Foundation.

Creating the Margin for Excellence

The Carolina First Campaign, the most successful fund-raising effort in University history, ends in three months well over the $2 billion goal. We exceeded that goal in February when we recorded the largest single pledge in UNC history, the $50 million commitment to the School of Public Health by Dennis and Joan Gillings. Our campaign total does not include the magnificent $100 million gift to the John Motley Morehead Foundation from the Gordon and Mary Cain Foundation, nearly doubling its endowment.

This morning, we announced an anonymous $5 million gift to benefit the honors program through five new endowed professorships to recognize Peter Grauer and William Harrison—alumni who have served Carolina with great distinction. That exceeds the campaign goal of creating 200 new endowed professorships. We are heading to the campaign's finish line with a special drive for faculty support, increasing that goal by an additional $100 million to $500 million.

For students, our donors have established 544 undergraduate scholarships and 188 graduate fellowships. Our endowment has surpassed $2 billion, over twice what it was seven-and-a-half years ago, a result of gifts and successful endowment management. These private funds are the fuel that is transforming this University, going from greatness to preeminence, to *be* the leading public university.

Transforming the Physical Campus

Our massive building program is adding 6 million square feet to the main campus. This program is grounded in core values of architectural quality and sustainability. The 2000 Higher Education Bonds brought $515 million for new buildings and renovations, and we more than kept our promise to triple this investment by North Carolina taxpayers. We have completed nearly 80 percent of those 49 bond projects and expect to finish in January 2009 within two months of our original projection—and on budget.

The total $2.1 billion building program, including projects funded by gifts, research grants, and our own revenues, is giving the campus community the physical space in which to excel in ways we have never been able before. The campus is being transformed. One of America's most beautiful campuses is becoming even more beautiful.

Carolina Connects: Serving North Carolina

Carolina has a long and cherished tradition of service to North Carolina, but we can and must do more. Vice Chancellor Mike Smith has formed the Carolina Engagement Council to help set our course, leading a campus dialogue on engaged scholarship. The Golden LEAF Foundation has committed at least $10 million over the next five years to support the faculty's work in rural communities across North Carolina.

Our ongoing work on this campus ties in naturally with the University of North Carolina Tomorrow Commission created by the Board of Governors and led by President Bowles. This commission is holding forums across the state to learn directly about community needs and how the UNC system can respond. We are continuing our own "Carolina Connects" initiative, launched in 2004, to listen to the people, to understand their needs, and to show what this University, with its statewide mission, is doing or ought to be doing to serve them. One thing we have learned is that we need to do a much better job of telling our story of how this University touches people's lives in all 100 counties of North Carolina on the issues that matter most to them—their health, the education of their children, and the economic prosperity of their region.

Advancing Carolina North: Our Future

Carolina North will be critical to our ability to help build the 21st century economy for North Carolina. Finally, after years of study and conversation, we are ready to begin. Later this afternoon, we expect the Board of Trustees to act on our plan for Carolina North. With their approval, we will begin the process of formal submission to the Town of Chapel Hill. We have identified our first building for Carolina North—an Innovation Center, where fledgling companies, using intellectual capital drawn from faculty research, can take their very first steps toward full viability. This partnership with a private developer, along with the new companies it creates, will pump new tax dollars into the community and support the local economy. Later, these new companies will create products and procedures that improve human health and the welfare of us all.

We have listened to the community and sought input from a broad spectrum over the past year. The Leadership Advisory Committee, chaired by former law dean and Chapel Hill Mayor Ken Broun, developed principles that have guided a series of draft concept plans presented to the community in meetings since last March. Carolina North's Executive Director, Jack Evans, and his colleagues have done an excellent job with this phase of work. The campus community and our neighbors have provided invaluable feedback, making the final concept blueprint better. The question of whether Carolina North will happen has been replaced by questions about how this mixed-use environment will function and how the University will consider the concerns and views of neighborhoods and the larger community.

At Carolina North, we will create strategic private-sector partnerships that will enable this University to be a more powerful force in the state's economy.

One issue closely related to Carolina North is our plan to close the Horace Williams Airport, which is where we will start the first phase of the new campus. Some see closing the airport as a lack of full support for the Area Health Education Centers (AHEC) Program. AHEC is the absolute anchor of this University's service to North Carolina, and the last thing we would ever do is diminish that service to communities, patients, and health professionals across the state. I firmly believe that we can both build Carolina North and strengthen AHEC.

In the near term, Medical Air Operations, the transportation arm of AHEC, will remain at Horace Williams until the Innovation Center is ready for occupancy. In the mid-term, Med Air will move to Raleigh-Durham Airport. We will work closely with AHEC physicians and staff to make that transition go smoothly.

In the long term, the University believes that a general aviation airport is important to the future of AHEC, the University itself, and to the economic success of Orange County. We pledge to work earnestly with local, state, and federal agencies to help create a general aviation authority for a new airport.

Bringing the World to North Carolina and Back

UNC has taken some critical steps toward becoming a great global university, bringing the world to North Carolina and taking North Carolina to the world. On University Day, October 12th, we will dedicate the FedEx Global Education Center and convene for the first time the Global Leadership Circle, a task force of visionary alumni leaders and friends, to help us develop a strategic vision for global engagement.

Last year, I went to China, where we co-sponsored a forum on health-care reform with Peking University. Next semester, we will host our Chinese colleagues at a similar conference focusing on health issues in the United States.

We are a world power in global health. Building on our faculty's historic strengths, we have launched the Institute for Global Health and Infectious Diseases, led by Dr. Mike Cohen. Through this institute, we will become even more effective in our research in infectious diseases, water quality and nutrition—work that is already improving and saving lives here and around the globe.

Ultimately, achieving our global objectives may be one of the most important things we do for our state. North Carolina's competition is not South Carolina or Georgia. It is Singapore . . . China . . . India. UNC must be a presence in the world so that North Carolina can compete in the world. It is as simple as that.

Looking Ahead: Challenges and Opportunities

Every part of the University is positioned for the kind of distinction that we expect at Carolina. We have come a long way, and I am pleased to report that the state of the University is excellent. However, I am not going to use my last year as chancellor for an extended victory lap. We have some real challenges to face. I want to do all I can this year to address the issues that, I believe, will dominate my successor's tenure. There are four major challenges.

Future Challenges: Growing to Serve North Carolina

First, enrollment growth will be, without question, the single most critical issue facing my successor. The UNC system expects to absorb approximately 80,000 additional students by 2017. Chapel Hill is already growing, and we will grow more to respond to the needs of an expanding and more diverse population seeking access to higher education in North Carolina. This is a huge challenge, and we must meet it. We cannot freeze-frame this University or embed it in amber. Rather we must continue to evolve and change to serve the public that created us and sustains us.

This fall, for the first time in our history, enrollment exceeded 28,000—about 4,000 more students than we had when I arrived seven years ago. Under our current trustee-approved plan from several years ago, enrollment will increase to nearly 30,000 by 2015. The question is, given what we know about the state's growth, will this be enough? And, if not, how will this University accommodate more?

The limiting factors for growth are resources and quality—resources for faculty and support staff; the necessary infrastructure of classrooms, offices, parking and transportation that allows the faculty to be a presence on the campus; and the amenities for student life that support the personal and social development of our students.

Quality is the other metric of control. We must ensure that admissions standards for undergraduates remain highly selective, and we must continue to push for higher graduation rates, which in itself will create more capacity. We must do nothing to degrade the quality of the entering class or of a Carolina degree. And we must increase support for graduate students, ensuring that Chapel Hill will continue to attract the world's finest young scholars to our graduate and professional programs. Indeed, it will be critical that we maintain the roughly 60–40 ratio of undergraduate to graduate and professional student population. This is crucial to the academic ecology of a research university.

I do not minimize the challenges that growth brings. While we should never compromise on quality, we and our successors must never send the message to the people who own this University that the door to opportunity has been closed.

This fall, we will undertake a comprehensive update of our campus master plan, beginning with a space needs assessment for various degrees of growth, to incorporate recent master planning by the UNC Health Care System and the School of Medicine, and to consider the possible programmatic uses of all our outlying properties, including Carolina North and Mason Farm.

Future Challenges: Competing in the Research Arena

The second most urgent challenge facing the University is the intensifying competition for research support.

In my installation address in 2000, I described the investment that we had just made in 18 faculty positions to support a new genomics initiative. That dramatic investment speaks for itself. Seven years later, UNC is a world leader in genomics and genetics research. Later, we made a similar investment in advanced materials science and nanotechnology.

Last year, I announced a goal of securing $1 billion in external research funding by 2015. It remains the audacious goal I described: "to take UNC to another level of excellence and prominence as a research university."[4]

To reach this goal, we must make some fundamental course adjustments. UNC has benefited enormously from the run-up of the NIH, but now we face a new federal reality—the decline in real dollars at NIH and a new federal escalator in the physical sciences, energy, and technology areas under legislation signed last month by President Bush. This initiative received initial Congressional funding this year and will ultimately double funding in these areas. One of the principal architects of this new federal thrust is Chancellor's Eminent Professor Dan Reed, who sits on the President's Council of Advisors on Science and Technology and chairs the policy board for the National Energy Research Scientific Computing Center.

To be successful in this new environment, we must make new strategic investments. We must increase our research capability in the physical sciences and build even more bridges between the biomedical and physical sciences. We must define new technical areas and approaches that create a competitive advantage for Carolina.

Simply put, we must devise a new strategy for innovation that builds on existing strengths, but that also includes recruiting and supporting new faculty who will foster multidisciplinary collaborations and lead new initiatives, both large and small.

I have asked Vice Chancellor Tony Waldrop to chair a faculty task force to develop a short list of big ideas for new investments.[5] The objective is to position Carolina to be successful in this new environment. This group will identify three to five broad thematic areas in which UNC will invest to increase its competitive position, taking into account existing strengths, as well as new opportunities. One of these broad themes has been given to us by the North Carolina General Assembly: cancer research.

Future Challenges: Finding Resources for New Investments

The third challenge will be to identify the resources for new investments. Let me be perfectly candid about what this means. Today, we could not make the investment in genomics that we did seven years ago because we do not have the resources available centrally. We have prided ourselves on placing our assets in a distributed manner, as close to the ground as possible. This has been an effective strategy for individual principal investigators to be successful in an environment of steadily increasing funding. It has maximized individual entrepreneurship. With this strategy of decentralized deployment and control, we have created internationally competitive departments, schools, centers, and institutes. However, there is a huge downside to this strategy when the rules of the game suddenly change—and they have suddenly changed. We have little ability to steer the ship to change its course.

Realistically, we cannot expect the state to provide all the new resources we will need for major new initiatives to the degree that it has done for cancer. We must find these resources internally. In a budget of over $2 billion, finding sufficient new investment capital should not be an insurmountable challenge, but it will challenge our traditional ways of doing business. Over the coming year, I shall ask the provost to develop with the deans a satisfactory method of capturing funds sufficient to allow some significant new investments in selected priority areas.

Future Challenges: Replenishing Faculty Resources

The fourth challenge is the essential resource of people—especially tenured and tenure-stream faculty—the people who do this research and provide service to the state. They are the key to everything. This is the supreme challenge.

According to a white paper by Bob Lowman, associate vice chancellor for research, nearly 41 percent of our faculty are 55 years of age or older.[6] Nationally, about half of all faculty leave the workforce by age 66, and 90 percent will have stopped working by age 70. (I should note that more and more faculty remain highly productive well into their 70s, a trend that I find myself applauding more and more. It is amazing how my own views about this have changed in the past few weeks.) Based on these national trends, we expect at least 500 tenured faculty members to retire in the next decade. That is more than double the rate of the past several years.

Besides those 500 new hires required by retirements, we will have to replace 1,300 faculty who will resign or not be reappointed, and find another 225 faculty to cover the current enrollment growth projection for 2015. That suggests, according to Lowman, "the need to recruit and hire approximately 2,000 new faculty members over the next eight years, or about 250 faculty per year."[7] This number does not include potential new faculty hires supported by the cancer research fund or accelerated enrollment growth.

To put these numbers in perspective, we now have nearly 3,300 full-time and part-time faculty. Hiring 2,000 faculty in eight years is the equivalent of replacing about five of every eight faculty.

The overwhelming prospect of replacing that many faculty is even more daunting when we remember that every other college and university in America will be facing similar problems of aging faculty, if not the same growth in enrollment.

This has huge implications. I suggest that we cannot approach this issue of faculty replenishment in the old mode of doing business—where departments and programs essentially clone the appointments made in the 1970s. In some cases, we may choose to replace a retiring specialist in the organ music of J.S. Bach with another Bach specialist, but I do not believe that even that position (which is probably mine, by the way) ought to be made without serious examination of larger alternatives.

Some of our major competitors are recruiting whole faculty teams, not just individuals. We have seen that in some of their raids on our best research groups. Clearly, they have an institutional strategic purpose in these recruitments. That is the nature of the game today, not only in big science. This is how we would build expertise in faculty with global or environmental perspectives, to name just two examples. Carolina has many individual strengths and an interdisciplinary culture that position us well to play in this game. Now, we need to take it to the next level.

This is a challenge and an opportunity to position UNC to realize its goal of being the leading public university—one of international preeminence.

Embracing Change and Holding Fast to Our Culture

There are a few advantages to having come late to Carolina with first-hand experience of other university cultures. This University is truly unique. It is a place that is open and free, that celebrates excellence wherever it occurs, that honors teaching and embraces selflessly a tradition of public service. We are a university with a healthy ego, but an innate modesty and lack of pretension. We take literally, sometimes too much so, I think, the motto of the State of North Carolina: Esse quam videri—to be, rather than to seem.

This is a place that, for many years, I held in high esteem from afar. I shall never forget the first time Susan and I walked on these brick paths eight years ago, knowing that we were about to have the high privilege of leading this great institution. I got goosebumps then. I still get them today.

This is a place we have come to love with every fiber of our being. I understand how it captures our students, who fall in love with it on their first visit; how, as World War II Veteran O.G. Grubbs wrote so beautifully in words inscribed in our new alumni memorial, "Chapel Hill is in my blood just as much as the sand and pebbles from the walks used to be in my shoes."[8]

I believe this University has the strength of character and maturity to embark on the bold and audacious initiatives I have described and not lose or endanger that wonderful culture of openness, freedom, civility, and collegiality. We love this place, but we must not let our love of it lead us to complacency and self-satisfaction. Once again, Carolina is called to lead—to lead change—to reinvent itself for the 21st century, holding fast to the incredible ethos of our bedrock values.

Over the course of the next year, I look forward to working with the trustees, provost, deans and faculty in addressing these critical issues that will, in my opinion, determine Carolina's future. My pledge to you is to bring the same level of passion, energy and commitment in my last year as I did in my first seven years as your chancellor.

Let us set the course so that a hundred years from now, historians will agree that Carolina's third century was her best, a true renaissance of the human spirit.

Notes

1. The *Carolina First Campaign*, which supported UNC's vision to be the nation's leading public university, began July 1, 1999, and ended Dec. 31, 2007. Its public launch came in October of 2002, with a $1.8 billion goal. That mark was raised to $2 billion in October of 2005. Not only did Carolina surpass its overall goal, raising $2.38 billion, but each professional school and unit exceeded individual goals as well. The campaign also boasted yearly records for commitments, topping out at $363.6 million (gifts and pledges) and $250.8 million (gifts) in fiscal year 2007.

The campaign received contributions from more than 190,000 donors, ranging from UNC students to Dennis and Joan Gillings, whose $50 million pledge to support the School of Public Health marked the single largest commitment in the University's history. The campaign's largest donor was the William R. Kenan, Jr. Charitable Trust and related Kenan entities and family members. They combined to contribute $69.9 million.

More than 700 campaign volunteers contributed their support, time, and expertise to make the drive a historic success.

To highlight just a few of the ways Carolina First moved Carolina forward, the campaign:

- brought in gifts that joined investment returns to increase UNC's endowment from $925.7 million to $2.2 billion, lifting UNC five spots in the *Chronicle of Higher Education's* rankings of U.S. university endowments as of June 30, 2007.
- created 208 endowed professorships, raising our total to 547.
- created 577 undergraduate scholarship funds, raising our total to 1,205.
- created 196 graduate fellowship funds, raising our total to 580.
- provided more than $100 million in support of 23 major building projects, including the purchase of Winston House in London for the European Study Center, UNC's first overseas property.

2. Carolina ranked first among top universities—for the sixth time in eight years—in the percentage of African-American students in the 2006 first-year class as measured by *The Journal of Blacks in Higher Education*. African-Americans made up 12.3 percent of that entering class – the second-highest percentage ever reported by the journal. Over the last decade, through 2006, Latino and Latina enrollment has quintupled, up 519 percent. Asian enrollment has grown by 68 percent. The fall 2007 first-year class includes 69.5 percent white students, down from 80 percent in 1997.

3. Current projections show the University is capable of reaching the 50th percentile this academic year in all areas except the School of Medicine, for which all peer data are not available.

4. Moeser, James. State of the University Address. Chapel Hill, N.C. Delivered on September 6, 2006.

5. Members of the strategic research planning task force, chaired by Tony Waldrop, vice chancellor for research and economic development, are: Shelton Earp, director, UNC Lineberger Comprehensive Cancer Center; Barbara Entwisle, director, Carolina Population Center; Daniel Reed, director of the Renaissance Computing Institute and Chancellor's Eminent Professor; and Holden Thorp, dean, College of Arts and Sciences.

6. Lowman, Robert. "Meeting the Challenge of a Changing Workforce." A white paper written about the University of North Carolina at Chapel Hill's future faculty workforce for internal discussion. Chapel Hill, N.C. May 29, 2007.

7. Lowman, Robert, p. 3.

8. Grubbs, O.J. Among the quotes featured as part of the "Carolina Alumni Memorial in Memory of Those Lost in Military Service," dedicated April 12, 2007, on the University of North Carolina at Chapel Hill campus.

THE TASK FOR LEADERSHIP: SUSTAINING RESEARCH
EXCELLENCE IN UNCERTAIN TIMES

Remarks for the Merrill Center Research Conference
The University of Kansas
July 21, 2010

IN JULY OF 2010, I was invited to present a paper on the subject of "Sustaining and Enhancing the Research Mission of Public Universities," at the Merrill Advanced Studies Center at the University of Kansas. I had made an earlier presentation at this center in 1997 when I was the Chancellor of the University of Nebraska-Lincoln.

This 2010 presentation serves as a concise summary of the goals, objectives, strategies, barriers, and accomplishments of my eight-year term as UNC Chancellor.

I WAS DELIGHTED TO receive the invitation to speak at this, the 14th annual research retreat sponsored by the Merrill Center for Advanced Studies at KU. I was privileged to attend and speak to the very first of these retreats in 1997, attending as the relatively new chancellor of the University of Nebraska-Lincoln. At that conference, my task was to be the clean-up hitter, listening to the presentations of faculty from the several institutions, summing up what I heard, and adding my own reflections in a piece I called "The Agenda for Change."

My task this time as the lead-off hitter is much more daunting, without the benefit of the shared wisdom of those of you in this room to draw on. It is our good fortune that I am followed in the line-up by two great hitters, Harvey Perlman and Bernadette Gray-Little, and I am confident of their ability to knock me in, provided I can get on base.

My charge from Mabel Rice is to articulate how top leaders can sustain research excellence for a public university in a time of fluctuating and uncertain public and financial support. She suggested that I might provide a list of the ten most useful things I learned about leading a research university, drawing most heavily from my eight years as chancellor of UNC Chapel Hill. In this paper, I will develop ten general principles, which I hope you will find helpful.

I believe that top leadership can impact the direction of a university; it can help create a climate that supports excellence in research; indeed, it can create a culture of excellence in an institution.

A savvy leader knows the history and culture of the institution, the state, and the region. Large universities turn like battle ships. Course corrections are possible, but only gradually, by increments.

We must always remember that a research university is a complex organization with a diffuse power structure. Presidents and chancellors lead by persuasion, not by fiat. Indeed, the more successful an institution is in attracting external funding, whether from peer-reviewed grants, foundations, or donors, the more decentralized the institution becomes. A highly successful faculty member can control more resources than many deans or department chairs.

As I began to think about these remarks, it occurred to me that I should review what I said back in 1997. Indeed, the first two principles I will give you this morning come from that earlier paper.

Paul Cheney, a distinguished KU neurophysiologist, made a compelling argument for lowering the walls that divide the many silos inside the academy. He quoted Mark Rogers, then the vice chancellor for health affairs at Duke, who wrote the following:

"The institutions that will succeed [in the future] are those that can reorganize themselves to address scientific and educational questions in an interdisciplinary manner. The institutions that will have difficulty are the ones that keep the same rigid structure that prevents pollination among disciplines."[1]

That concept became a mantra for me at Nebraska and later at North Carolina. The more I realized the futility of attempting to dismantle hardened walls, the more I began to use the language of biology to speak of walls that were more like permeable membranes.

However one characterizes it, this is an essential culture for a successful research university.

Eli Michaelis, the chair of KU's pharmacology and toxicology department, spoke eloquently about the two factors that drive successful researchers: uncertainty and urgency. He also spoke candidly and revealingly about his own fear of failure, observing that the most audacious objectives carried with them the greatest risk of failure. I distilled a principle out of this that I applied to my own objectives for two universities: the greater the attempt, the greater the reward, and also the greater the risk of failure. It is this sobering realization, however, that often leads to the ultimate failure of leadership—the failure to act. Institutions that coast are, by definition, on a down-hill track.

I arrived in Chapel Hill in August of 2000 at a precipitous moment in the history of this, the oldest public university in America. The campus was showing its age. After years of neglect from the state, deferred maintenance was at an alarming stage. Our world-class chemistry department was still teaching and doing research in a 1925 building. The music library, one of the three strongest research collections in America, was housed in a basement of an old Carnegie Library with leaking pipes running overhead. I was replacing a chancellor who had died in office, leaving a substantial structural budgetary deficit. I had to find a provost, a chief financial officer, and a chief research officer.

To counterbalance these problems (which I saw as opportunities) were many positives. First, I discovered an incredibly positive faculty culture. Unlike my experience at three other universities, where the best faculty had opted out of governance, some of UNC's most distinguished faculty were highly active in governance and eager to work with a new chancellor. It was not uncommon for the faculty chair to be a member of one of the national academies. UNC was recognized in the then just-released Lombardi ranking of research universities as one of only four public research universities in the top tier along with Berkeley, Michigan, and UCLA.

I quickly realized that the strategies I had employed at Nebraska, and earlier as provost at South Carolina, with significant reallocation of funds from marginal areas to concentrated and focused areas of excellence, would be inappropriate for a university with very few areas that could be called weak, and many that were excellent and highly regarded. I adopted a strategy that we would have a low tolerance for marginal programs, which meant, with a small number of such programs, we could afford to move resources to shore them up.

(If there is a principle that can be distilled here, I believe it is this: In developing institutional strategic objectives, one must always begin with an honest institutional assessment. I strongly believe in setting high goals, but those goals need to be grounded in reality).

On the November 2000 ballot was a $3.2 billion higher education construction bond issue, of which $525 million was slated to go to Chapel Hill. In my installation address in October, I took a deep breath and pledged to the voters that we would triple that investment in private fund raising if they would approve the bonds. (We were on the cusp of announcing a billion dollar-plus capital campaign, but I had great anxiety about our ability to raise that kind of money. This is an example of my earlier point about the fear of failure.)

Timing is everything—in hand grenades, music, and politics. In November of 2000, the dot-com bust was still over the horizon. People were optimistic. The voters approved the bond issue with a 75% plurality, passing in all 100 counties. It stands, still to this day, as the largest higher education construction bond ever passed by any state. Fortunately, because of the success of the Carolina First Campaign, which ultimately raised $2.38 billion for academic support including 225 endowed chairs, nearly a thousand new scholarships and fellowships, and significant commitments to facilities for research, I was able to relax. At the end of the day, we had increased the state's investment five-fold.

I realized that this was a critical moment in the history of this university. UNC was highly ranked, but also highly vulnerable, due to these obvious deficiencies in the infrastructure and relatively low faculty salaries. Instinctively, I felt that this was the right time for a major investment in big science. We had obvious strengths on which to build, and I knew that it would be a fatal mistake to begin my first big efforts in my own playground of the arts and humanities. I also realized that I needed a really strong internal leadership team to develop a strategy. With my lack of background in science, I needed senior colleagues with strong research credentials. So, I recruited Robert Shelton, the vice president for research of the University of California, a physicist and former department chair at UC-Davis, to be provost. We recruited Tony Waldrop, the vice chancellor for research at Illinois, to take the same position at UNC. (When Shelton left after several years to become president of the University of Arizona, I named Bernadette Gray-Little, the dean of the College and now KU's chancellor, to be our provost.) I always had a strong colleague in that essential office.

We decided that the capital construction program, which over eight years grew to $2.2 billion and more than 6 million new square feet, would be front-end loaded with research and teaching facilities for the physical sciences, medicine, public health, and pharmacy. We drafted our leading research faculty into planning teams for these new buildings. (The ability to dream and then build new facilities is one of the strongest retention devices I know.) We also used these new facilities, even in the planning stages, as the hooks for recruiting new faculty. Every area of the university was affected by this infusion of support, but none more than the physical science departments of the College—chemistry, physics and astronomy, marine science, biology, and computer science.

Early on, in my very first year, when we were fortunate enough to receive a huge bolus of new faculty lines due to enrollment growth, we made the critical decision to hold back 18 lines for a new investment in genomics to create the Carolina Center for Genome Sciences, with faculty appointments from seven different academic units representing over 15 departments and disciplines. To chair a new department of genetics in the School of Medicine, we recruited Terry Magnuson from Case Western Reserve University. He brought with him his 15-member research group, and 10,000 mice. Magnuson is a preeminent geneticist who could have gone anywhere but chose Carolina because he was attracted by the idea of creating a really big center. Candidly, another part of the attraction was the fact that we promised him a building. Ultimately, we built two massive research buildings, with still two more on the way. Terry now helps us recruit new faculty telling them, "these people make promises, and they deliver. They keep their word."

What are the lessons from this experience that I can pass on to you as principles? First, physical facilities matter. We are, indeed, in an arms race of facilities, and the best faculty will migrate to the places that provide them the tools to do their best work. That means state-of-the art equipment. But it also means flexible space that is well designed to maximize human interaction.

We designed our buildings with connecting bridges and with meeting spaces and break-out rooms along the corridors and even in the bridges to encourage and facilitate the occasional "aha" moments that sometimes lead to creative breakthroughs. Our goal was that this science complex would allow one to walk through all the science departments in the College to the health science schools in one continuum.)

The corollary principle, one that I articulated in 1997, is this: faculty should be recruited in clusters, not just one at a time. The really big questions cross all the traditional boundaries. This means that departments can no longer exercise complete autonomy over hiring. I don't mean to suggest a totally top-down process for hiring decisions, but rather a negotiated process involving the provost and the top leadership.

To pursue such a strategy requires a plan, an architecture for strategic investment. Once I had the leadership team in place, I charged the provost with the development of an academic plan, which we adopted in July of 2003. A good plan needs to be specific enough to include concrete action steps, assignment of responsibility and a mechanism for measuring success. It also needs to be flexible enough to allow for opportunistic adjustments as the environment evolves.

Building Public Support

As I think back on my eight years in the chancellor's office, I am struck by how much of my time and effort was devoted to building public support for the university's research mission. We learned much from the successful campaign in the fall of 2000 to pass the higher education construction bond. We learned that there was a large reservoir of support for the university among the people of North Carolina. They loved us, but they knew very little about what we do or how we contribute to the betterment of their existence, other than the education of their sons and daughters. That told us we had some major work to do in telling our story.

That also translated into problems we had in the state legislature. For years, the state and/or the university system had been reducing our state appropriation by a percentage (up to 25%) of our federal F&A receipts, with the mistaken view that the campus was adequately compensated for its conduct of research, and these state funds constituted "double dipping." (This, of course, reflects a total misunderstanding of the inadequacy of the federal F&A rate, which needs no discussion here.)

I helped our Board of Trustees understand how critical reversing this practice was to advancing the university's research agenda. We had an urgent case in the construction of the science complex, where a portion of the first phase was going to be shelled-in without additional resources. (The state had included a private fund-raising component for every one of our projects that received the total $525 million in bond funds.) We needed to build out the shelled space in order to retain a key faculty member who was being heavily recruited by several other universities, but we had not yet raised the private funds. We devised a plan to finish the space by using F&A funds to back-stop future private fund-raising. But that plan would fail, if the state, in effect, took part of our F&A away.

Our board mobilized and formed a political action committee, which in a short period of time became one of the most powerful political lobbies in North Carolina, the second largest political action group in the state. The PAC's existence and effectiveness were not always appreciated by the system administration and board, and it was regularly attacked in the editorial pages of the local press as it grew more and more powerful.

The PAC quickly made a legislator's position on F&A retention as the proxy for being a friend of Chapel Hill and thus meriting the PAC's support. Gradually, the climate on our retention of F&A receipts began to change. I recall the first time I had to testify before a legislative committee, facing open skepticism about our plans for using F&A receipts to leverage research growth.

I decided to try to disarm them with a little self-deprecating humor saying, "Proteomics, Genomics, . . . all these '-omics.' What do I know about them? I'm only a humble village organist." This seemed to work. They smiled and relaxed and began to listen. The point I really wanted to make is that we intended to use F&A receipts, including anticipated receipts on future research, as front-end cash to build out our research facilities, to back-stop anticipated private fund-raising.

Fortunately, over time, we began to win those arguments. While I would like to think it was the force and logic of our argument that won the day, I cannot discount the political power of the PAC. However, it was not all brute political force. Gradually, we began to succeed in connecting research to economic development, a powerful argument for state support. We marshaled the support of the major private sector research-based firms in Research Triangle Park, many of which had their origins in university-based research. The CEOs of these firms contributed directly to the PAC, and they spoke up for us in the legislature.

Gradually, we turned the tide on F&A receipts, and in a couple of years there were no more recorded votes on UNC's F&A receipts. We were free of any state or system control with regard to their usage, allowing us to use F&A funds to finish space in the new science complex that would have otherwise been shelled-in, creating research space that enabled us to win a fierce battle to retain a key scientist. With this dedicated space and about ten new faculty lines, we established a new Institute for Advanced Materials, Nanoscience, and Technology. I recall that the year we did this, 2002, was a particularly difficult year, in which we were facing budget cuts, and I took some political risk in making such a bold move in an otherwise down year. In my State of the University address that year, I said this:

> Some will argue that we cannot afford new initiatives in the current environment. I would respond that, while we must be very judicious in taking on new projects, we cannot afford not to build on our strengths to be the very best that we can be. I think we should all agree on one thing—that we will start nothing that we are not willing to support sufficiently to make it a top-10 program within a reasonable period of time. We must be willing to pull the plug of life support on new programs that fail to meet that threshold.[2]

This was an investment that paid off. Within five years, UNC was in the top ten nationally based on NSF funding in this area, competing with universities all of which had big engineering schools.

Between 2000 and 2009, UNC plowed $43 million in F&A funds directly into research facilities, and another $90 million into debt service on research construction with an asset valuation of $236 million.

What began as a defensive strategy to protect our F&A receipts gradually evolved into a continuing program of advocacy for the university and its research enterprise. By the end of my tenure, we were coming to the end of the funding stream from the Higher Education Construction Bond, and yet our needs and aspirations had expanded. Also, by this time, we had established strong relationships with the political leadership in the North Carolina Senate, who had become strong supporters, some would say patrons, of UNC's research enterprise. In fairly rapid succession, the North Carolina legislature funded a new UNC Cancer Hospital ($180 M), a new research building for the School of Dentistry, and a bio-medical imaging building ($350 M), the last in a year when there was no other capital construction funding anywhere else in the state. However, the most stunning demonstration of the legislature's support for UNC research was the appropriation in 2008 of $50 million in continuing funding for cancer research. UNC is effectively leveraging that funding stream to increase its funding from federal sources.

The point to be made here is the importance of building public and political support in our respective states for the research enterprise of a public research university. We should capitalize on our status as flagship institutions and make the case to state policy makers that we are the principal drivers of innovation that leads to economic development and job creation. This case is easier to make today than it was ten years ago. We should never apologize for being research universities; we should never apologize for research, but rather celebrate it and find ways to connect our research to people's lives.

One of the clearest paths of connection to people's lives is through our educational outreach programs. At UNC, the Morehead Planetarium and Science Center has long been the center of our outreach for children and youth. One out of three North Carolinians under the age of 18 has visited the Morehead on campus. Thousands more have benefitted from the "science bus" that takes hands-on science experiences to North Carolina high schools. Next fall, the Morehead will sponsor a two-week science festival, with 139 events in 57 locations across the state. Our goal is to put the spotlight on science, to do for science in the 21st century what state fairs did for agriculture in the 20th. We believe that this is a model that can be adopted by other states, and we are inviting people from other states to come as observers. While this is not designed as a public relations tool, we believe this festival can have a powerful effect in building public support for what we do.

The North Carolina story is one that can be replicated in other states. Strong state support can leverage strong federal support and strong private support, and vice versa. Each of these is mutually reinforcing of the others.

Public Support for Faculty Salaries

If there was a single thread that ran through all my public presentations during my tenure, it was the importance of faculty salaries. We made faculty support the number one priority of the Carolina First Campaign, creating 225 endowed professorships. It was also the centerpiece of our legislative efforts as well.

I convinced the Board of Trustees of the importance of recruiting and retaining the best faculty as the centerpiece of all we were attempting to do. They got it. The PAC got it, and they were enormously helpful. Once we won the F&A battle, faculty salaries became the issue.

I won't belabor this issue, because you all understand the importance of faculty support to furthering the research agenda. The point I want to make here is that this is an argument that one must win with the public and with policy makers.

We fought this battle on three fronts—in the legislature, for state appropriations; with the system over the right to raise tuition when the state was unable to provide salary increases; and as the centerpiece of the fund-raising effort.

I used to say that we wanted to have a faculty that the University of Chicago wanted. The trouble is that the University of Chicago (and their several peers) came calling. In 2003, we discovered that we were losing two out of three contested counter-offers. This was a clear path to mediocrity. It was a crisis. We were at a difficult time in terms of state support, with several years of little or no increases in faculty compensation.

North Carolina has a long tradition of low tuition coupled with generous state support. When that support went into decline, however, it was critical that we turn to tuition as a funding source for faculty salaries. We succeeded in getting authorization from the legislature to increase tuition and to keep those funds on campus for faculty support and need-based student aid. Simultaneously, we created the Carolina Covenant program, which guaranteed all students at or below 200% of the federal poverty level, a debt-free graduation. This program became a national model.

Even with these safeguards in place, I still had major battles with the system Board of Governors, which had little sympathy for the plight of its flagship research campus and no understanding of the competitive environment for research universities. Once again, the PAC came to our rescue, convincing the legislature to overrule the system board. Perhaps my most telling argument to them was the fact that UNC faculty across the university averaged $211,000 in external funding, while the average salary was about $165,000. Talk about a return on investment, this was it!

Three years later, as a result of salary increases funded largely from tuition sources, we had reversed the negative trend, winning two out of every three contested retentions. By the time I left office, after two very good years of state appropriations, UNC's faculty salaries, by rank, were higher than either Michigan or Virginia, and only slightly behind UC Berkeley and UCLA, our four major national peers. This was a key part of our overall strategy, and I am convinced our success with regard to faculty compensation was directly related to the success of our research effort. The run-up in research funding at UNC is an impressive story. External research at UNC increased from $375 million in 2000 to $716 million in 2009, and as of June 30, 2010, has just crossed the $800 million threshold.

Vision

In 2003, when the NIH Roadmap initiative was first announced, we commissioned a team of our best scientists, some of whom had just been recruited in the early wave of faculty appointments, to plan for the Roadmap, which itself, would map the future of NIH initiatives. As a result of this initiative, UNC led the nation with the number of Roadmap awards in the first year and again in the second.

We were totally opportunistic in this case. We were fortunate that our strengths mapped well with where we thought the NIH wanted to go, and we put major resources into place in order to be competitive. Given the investment the state was also making in research infrastructure and, later, direct research support, we could leverage each of these elements constructively.

Here, perhaps, I can derive another principle. To be successful in big science, institutions need to think strategically, placing bets by allocating resources where there may be a big return. This requires a certain degree of central planning, just as we did with the NIH roadmap. To be sure, a successful university will always have a balance of individual PI grants and some big team-based grants. But the major leagues are dominated by the latter, not the former. This requires us to be brutally honest about our capabilities. There are some big opportunities out there that we simply do not have the resources to address. No amount of incremental funding would matter. We have to be willing to say no to investment in such ideas, attractive as they may be to one or more advocates. This is a critical point. Great universities do not dabble in areas where they lack strength or competence. It is important to know when to say no, to have the courage to say it, and to stick with your decision.

In 2006, in my fall State of the University address, I hit the campus with a blockbuster. With external funding at just short of $600 million, I proposed establishing a goal of $1 billion in external funding by 2015. I arrived at this number in close consultation with Tony Waldrop, the vice chancellor for research, who assured me that, while this was a huge stretch goal, it was not impossible. This is what I said:

Let us be crystal clear about this: $1 billion is a stretch goal, more than $200 million above what we might be expected to reach at our current trajectory. Some have argued that this is too high... unrealistic... that the uncompensated cost of this research will be unaffordable. To use a Jim Collins term, this is a "big, hairy, audacious goal," appropriate for a university aspiring to be the leading public university. We should dream no small dreams.[3]

Sometimes it is important for a leader to lay out something like this, without the assurance of success, remembering that big goals carry with them the high risk of failure. Just as I did not have absolute confidence in my promise in 2000 that we would triple the people's investment in the bond issue, and I am not certain that UNC will reach this goal. But I am certain that it is on a positive trajectory to do exactly that, and, in my opinion, that is all that matters.[4]

I believe that this is one of the major responsibilities of leadership: to set a vision, and to be the principal cheer-leader for that vision.

Over time, I discovered that one of the things state policy makers could quickly grasp was the connection between research, tech transfer, and job creation. When I arrived in Chapel Hill, UNC had a dismal record of creating spin-offs; the tech transfer office was seen as a barrier, rather than a bridge; the institutional culture was anything but supportive of entrepreneurship. We worked hard to change that culture.

My partner in this effort was Tony Waldrop, the vice chancellor for research, whose title we changed to research and economic development. We beefed up the tech transfer office, brought in new leadership, and we listened to our most entrepreneurial faculty about what they wanted and needed. I made a key change in the Office of General Counsel, another office that was regarded as a major obstacle.

Over time, we saw a complete transformation of the culture for tech transfer from negative to positive. In 2004 UNC received one of seven grants in a national competition from the Ewing M. Kauffman Foundation to embed entrepreneurship into the curriculum. By placing this new program as an undergraduate minor in the College, rather than in the Business School, we were able to impact the entire campus. As a result, today we have programs in social entrepreneurship, and artistic entrepreneurship, not just the usual suspects from science, technology, and the health professions. The culture really did change.

However, as I left office in 2008, I could still occasionally hear complaints from our faculty about the pace of tech transfer. We still were not where we needed to be for our most ambitious faculty entrepreneurs. In December of 2009, Tony Waldrop and his colleagues announced a real breakthrough that Cathy Innes, UNC's director of the Office of Technology Development, called "the Holy Grail in technology transfer transactions—the standard license agreement." The Carolina Express License[5] offers the same terms to all UNC start-ups and offers the best deal available from the University, covering a widely divergent stream of deal-flow with minimal negotiation. I can't claim any credit for this development, which occurred after I left office, except to say that it all started with a fundamental policy shift to be an entrepreneurial university. In my opinion, this is where research universities need to be, especially public universities. That is at least a part of our raison d'être as servants of society.

This focus on economic development and job creation needs to be kept in focus and in balance. It is a hand that can easily be overplayed, and this is a trap that must be avoided. It cannot become the only metric for success. There is a second trap here that is especially tempting for trustees, and that is to make the funding stream from licensing fees the goal. Everybody wants the next Gatorade. The new Carolina Express License actually makes concessions on this point, sacrificing some short-term financial return in favor of more rapid spin-off creation.

Finally, I must speak about the arts and humanities. I am personally sensitive to this area, because it is my own. I was acutely aware that in my first five years at UNC, much of my time and energy was spent on big science, medicine, and technology. These were areas of critical concern and major opportunity.

However, I was also aware of the fact that I presided over a university with a distinguished history in the arts, humanities, and social sciences. In fact, one of Carolina's strengths was the balance among each of these major areas. I regarded that history as a treasure that I was determined to preserve and protect.

One of the early decisions that Provost Shelton and I made together when the budget cuts began early in the decade was that, at all costs, we were going to protect the library. Not the serials budget, but the acquisitions and operations budget of the library.

As time passed and our position became more and more secure, we turned gradually to providing more direct support to the arts and humanities. We made a major investment in the performing arts presenting program, for example. We made sure that some F&A resources were directed to small grants programs for faculty in the arts and humanities. We went out of our way to celebrate individual faculty accomplishments—election to one of the national academies, appointments to endowed chairs. We raised some serious private money to support these areas.

Here is the principle I want to evoke: A great research university must maintain a balance, an equilibrium, between those areas that garner major external funding, and those that never will. Core areas of strength in key areas of the arts, humanities, and social sciences must be maintained. This requires a certain sophistication in the internal funding model, openness and transparency in the flow of funds, but above all, the strength and courage of top leadership to do what is necessary to support faculty research and creative activity in these areas.

Let me conclude by simply summarizing the basic principles I have outlined in this paper, going back to my 1997 presentation.

- Lower the walls of the silos to facilitate inter-disciplinary work. Create inter- and multi-disciplinary research clusters to address large problems.
- The greater the attempt, the greater the reward, and the greater risk for failure. Fear of failure often leads to the greatest failure of leadership—the failure to act.
- In developing institutional strategic objectives, one must always begin with an honest institutional assessment. I strongly believe in setting high goals—big, hairy, audacious goals, but those goals need to be grounded in reality.
- Facilities matter. We are, indeed, in an arms race. Good research facilities are a magnet for faculty and graduate students.
- Faculty have to be recruited in clusters in order to create major new initiatives, in addition to traditional departmental replacement hires. This requires an overall architecture for strategic investment.
- Strong support from the state for research can leverage stronger federal and private support. We must never apologize for research, but rather celebrate it and find ways to connect it to people's lives.

- Public support for faculty compensation is vital. Faculty compensation is the most critical area of national competition. Everything hangs on the quality of the faculty.
- To be successful in big science, institutions need to think strategically, placing bets by allocating resources where there may be a big return. The major responsibility of top leadership is to set a vision and to be the cheerleader-in-chief in articulating that vision to the university's many constituencies.
- A culture of entrepreneurship is a critical value. Success in economic development and job creation is the best argument for continued support for research. Avoid the traps. Don't overplay this hand. This must not be the only metric of success. The funding stream from licensing is not the goal.
- A great research university must maintain a balance, an equilibrium, between those areas that garner major external funding, and those that never will. It is a primary responsibility of top leadership to maintain areas of strength in key areas of the arts, humanities, and social sciences. This takes vision and courage.

Notes

1. Mark Rogers. The Scientist. 1995
2. James Moeser, State of the University Address, September 4, 2002
3. James Moeser, State of the University Address, September 6, 2006.
4. UNC reached the goal, on schedule, in 2015.
5. "UNC unveils innovative new licensing model to spur business spin-offs," UNC press release, December 10, 2009.

REMARKS FOR THE UNVEILING OF THE PORTRAIT

The University of North Carolina at Chapel Hill
October 7, 2011

My only major campus address as Chancellor Emeritus was the unveiling of my portrait. The Ceremony was held in Memorial Hall, one of the most special places on the Carolina campus for Susan and me. This address was an opportunity to express my deep love and appreciation for Carolina and the arts and humanities.

CHANCELLOR THORP, FRIENDS, AND GUESTS,

This is a special moment for Susan and for me, and we deeply appreciate that so many of our friends and colleagues could be here this afternoon to share this event with us. As I look out over this crowd, I am ever so conscious of the fact that everyone in this room is part of the Carolina story of the first decade of the 21st century.

Roger,[1] thank you so much for your kind words. Your leadership of the Board of Trustees is one of the high points of that story. Holden, your rapid rise through the ranks is another part of that story. I appreciate that you brought Susan up to the podium to share in this moment, because she was as thrilled as I was when we first came to UNC in the late summer of 2000. She has walked with me every step of the way.

When this portrait is hung in Wilson Library, it will join a great procession of my predecessors—Robert House, William Aycock, Paul Sharp, Carlyle

Sitterson, Ferebee Taylor, Chris Fordham, Paul Hardin, and Michael Hooker. I am so pleased that Paul and Barbara Hardin could be present today.

I am pleased that John Howard Sanden, the portrait artist, painted me in front of Daniel Chester French's *Spirit of Life* sculpture, which stands at the center inside the entrance to Wilson Library, just to the right of the row of portraits. He chose this setting, he said, in order to depict my love of music, my first love and first professional calling, and this university's commitment to the arts and humanities.

I like to think of this sculpture as representing the spirit of Carolina, a university with a proud, if imperfect history, rising from the same springs as the American Revolution; defending constitutional liberties; leading the South into the modern age; becoming one of the great research universities of the world in the late 20th century with the audacious vision of being America's leading public university—all this while maintaining the essential humility and grace of its more modest creation by the people of a state whose motto is *Esse quam videre*: to be rather than to seem. This is a proudly public university—the university of the people as coined by Charles Kuralt, yet a university with such a devoutly spiritual core that Gerrard Hall, the 1822 chapel right next door, has the words of Micah inscribed on it: "Do justice, love mercy, and walk humbly with thy God."

Thus, it was innate to our culture for the Carolina Covenant, which led the way for almost a hundred other institutions to create programs that guarantee a debt-free education to low-income students, to spring forth here. It was innate to our culture for Carolina to make a strong commitment to diversity and inclusion, to focus on the critical social issues of the times, racism, poverty, sexual orientation and identity. It was innate to our culture that Carolina was the first major institution to end binding early decision admissions, recognizing that students from the least affluent backgrounds were disadvantaged by this practice. Many followed us at the time, and sadly, many have also quietly reverted to their old practices while few were watching. It was innate to our culture that in the wake of 9/11, we should ask our students to read a book about the Qur'an, and it was equally innate that we should defend that choice against all attacks, just as Bill Aycock and Bill Friday had defended free speech against the Speaker Ban Law.

I appreciate that we are in my favorite space on this campus—Memorial Hall, which symbolizes this university's great commitment to the arts, recognizing that a truly great university must have excellence in science and medicine, but also in the social sciences, the humanities, and the arts. I think this is the secret to Carolina's greatness—that with all our investments and our success with big science, including a promising new investment in applied science, we continue to value and support the arts and humanities. This is why the Mellon Foundation, which just awarded $750,000 to Carolina Performing Arts for a signature celebration of the 100th anniversary of Stravinsky's *Rite of Spring*, told us that UNC is the one public university that still celebrates the humanities.

When Susan and I were in South Carolina, we had the privilege of getting to know the late poet, James Dickey. We invited Dickey to give the commencement address one year at South Carolina, and I still have that speech in my library, it was so memorable. In it he recounted the story of the famous debate in the Oxford Union over a century and a half ago between Thomas Henry Huxley, the biologist and public defender of Darwin, and Matthew Arnold, the poet and Professor of Poetry at Oxford. These are Dickey's words:

> "Huxley contended that the future of education lay in confining the curriculum to technological subjects. These exclusively were to be taught, for the wave of the future was to be science, and education should recognize this and mold people to take their places within a culture not only dominated by science but created by it. [...] His opponent in the debate, Matthew Arnold, took the opposite view: the purpose of education, he said, is not to condition people to interrelate with machines [...] but to aid the student in becoming a certain kind of person, an individual with his own needs and potentialities, perhaps including scientific preoccupations but not limited to them." Dickey continued, "it seems to me that Huxley was partially right, but that Arnold was entirely right. Arnold believed, with the poet John Keats, that life is a vale of soul-making. He thought that life was given to him to find the right use of it, that it was a kind of continuous magical confrontation [...] derived from intuition, courage, and the accumulation of experience. It was not a formula of any kind, not a piece of rationality, but rather a way of being and of acting."[2]

That is as good a description of a liberal arts education as you will ever find. It describes this place—a vale of soul-making.

So when you look at this portrait, do not fail to see Daniel Chester French's *Spirit of Life* in the background. That is the spirit of this place, this university that we love, this Carolina.

Notes

1. Roger Perry, Chair, Board of Trustees.
2. James Dickey. "The Weather of the Valley: Reflections on the Soul and Its Making." Commencement address at the University of South Carolina, Columbia, SC, August 11, 1990.

INDEX

Academic Advising Program, 68
Academy of Distinguished Teaching Scholars, 8
Ackland Art Museum, 21, 88
Advisory Committee on the Economic Conditions of the South, 65
AHEC Clinic, 64
Alexander Residence Hall, 100
APPLES, 22
Area Health Education Centers Program, 64, 80, 82, 112
Arnold, Matthew, 139
Aycock, William, 2, 23, 33, 35, 36, 106, 137, 138

Bach, JS, 117
Basnight, Marc, 107
Battle, Kemp, 2
Baxter, Stephen, 68
Bollenbacher, Skip, 58
Boucher, Richard, 18
Bowers, Terry, 106
Bowles, Erskine, 95, 96, 99, 106, 108, 109, 111
Broad, Molly Corbett, 52, 53
Broun, Ken, 112
Brown-Graham, Anita, 65
Browning, Christopher, 93
Bush, George W., 115

C. Knox Massey Distinguished Service Awards, 68, 99, 106

Campus Development Plan, 11
Cannon, Carolyn, 106
Carnegie Library, 123
Carolina Center for Genome Sciences, 125
Carolina Center for Public Service, 8, 82
Carolina Computing Initiative, 8, 73
Carolina Connects, 63, 64, 66, 111
Carolina Covenant, 49, 53, 66, 67, 84, 87, 100, 105, 108, 130, 138
Carolina Engagement Foundation, 111
Carolina Express License, 133
Carolina First Campaign, 34, 39, 42, 44, 49, 52, 57, 67, 70, 71, 86, 87, 93, 95, 105, 110, 124, 129
Carolina North, 45, 73, 74, 77, 81, 82, 86, 87, 88, 102, 105, 111, 112, 114
Carolina Performing Arts Series, 88, 89, 139
Carolina Postdoctoral Program for Faculty Diversity, 84
Carolina Union, 100
Carroll Hall, 21
Caulberg, Sandra, 68
Center for the Study of the American South, 46
Chambers, Julius, 46
Chancellor's Student Awards, 13
Chase, Harry Woodburn, 2, 5
Cheney, Paul, 122
Citizen-Solider Initiative, 74

INDEX

Clark, Fred, 84, 100
Coates, Albert, 40
Coclanis, Peter, 80
Cohen, Mike, 113
Coffin, William Sloane, 36
College of Arts and Sciences, 7, 22, 41, 49, 52, 68, 71, 74, 101
Collins, Francis, 7
Collins, Jim, 91, 92, 97, 132
Committee on Student Conduct, 43
Crowder, Timm, 18

Darwin, Charles, 139
Davie, William Richardson, 1, 10, 103
DePaolo, Rosemary, 75
Department of Music, 21
Department of Physics and Astronomy, 94
DeSimone, Joe, 17
Destiny and Discovery, 82
Dickey, James, 139
Duderstadt, James, 50, 51

Easley, Mike, 50, 69, 107
Egerton, John, 30, 40
Ehrenreich, Barbara, 49
Elfland, Carolyn, 20
Employee Forum, 21, 63
Ervin, Archie, 73, 85, 100
Estroff, Sue, 12, 13
European Study Center, 97
Evans, Jack, 102

Facilities Services Division, 68
Faculty Council, 21, 43
FedEx Global Education Center, 113
First Year Seminars, 52
Fitzgerald, Jill, 64
FitzGerald, Kevin, 65

Five Year Financial Plan, 93
Flagler, Mary Lily Kenan, 2
Fordham, Christopher, 2, 36, 106, 138
Foy, Kevin, 59
Franklin Street, 59
French, Daniel Chester, 138, 139
Friday, Bill, 2, 12, 23, 33, 35, 36, 138
Friedman, Thomas, 79

Gardner, Alston, 78
Gerrard Hall, 47, 88, 138
Gillings, Dennis, 110, 119
Gillings, Joan, 110, 119
Global Education Center, 58, 77, 80, 97
Global Leadership Circle, 113
Godschalk, David, 68
Gold, Stuart, 64
Gomes, Peter, 46
Gordon and Mary Cain Foundation, 110
Graham, Edward Kidder, 2, 5, 22, 40, 58
Graham, Frank Porter, 2, 5, 10, 12, 13, 14, 23, 33, 35, 47, 65, 93
Griffin, Tommy, 57, 63, 67
Grauer, Peter, 110
Gray-Little, Bernadette, 99, 121, 124
Grounds Services Department, 106
Grubbs, OG, 118
Guillory, Ferrel, 30

Hackney, Joe, 107
Hackney, Ray, 100
Haislip, Josh, 94
Hardin, Barbara, 138
Hardin III, Paul, 2, 36, 106, 138
Harrison, William, 110
Helms, Jesse, 30
Higher Education Construction Bond, 128

Highway Safety Research Center, 74
Honors Program, 42, 52, 71
Hooker, Michael xiii, 3, 4, 138
Hooker-Odum, Carmen, 3
Horace Williams Airport, 81, 112
House, Robert, 137
Human Genome Project, 7
Hunt, Jim, 30
Huxley, Thomas Henry, 139

Innes, Cathy, 133

Innovation Center, 112
Institute for Advanced Materials, Nanoscience and Technology, 45, 128
Institute for Global Health and Infectious Diseases, 90, 113
Institute for Renaissance Computing, 72, 97, 101
Institute of Arts and Humanities, 46
Institute of Government, 82
Institute of Marine Sciences, 65

Ishaq, Khalid, 18

James, Thomas, 83
Jefferson, Thomas, 1, 75
John Motley Morehead Foundation, 110
Johnson, Jim, 65
Jones, Ben, 45

Keats, John, 139
Keith, Larry, 100
Kenan-Flagler Business School, 22, 46, 65
Kenan Professorships, 2
Kenan Stadium, 108
Klapper, Sue, 106
Ko, Esther, 100

Koh, Tommy, 78
Kuralt, Charles, 92, 99, 138
Kwon, Jin Yi, 64

Leadership Advisory Committee, 102, 112
LEARN North Carolina, 82
Lee, Bard, 78
Lee, Howard, 83, 84
Lineberger Comprehensive Cancer Center, 58, 69, 106
Lowman, Bob, 116, 117
Lowry and Susan Caudill Laboratories, 93
Lucido, Jerry, 54
Luettich, Rick, 65
Luse, Don, 100

Magnuson, Terry, 125
Mason Farm, 20, 114
Massey, C. Knox, 68
McCoy, William, 3, 36, 106
Measures of Excellence, 34
Medical Air Operations, 80, 81, 112
Memorial Hall, 88, 89, 137, 138
Micah, 10, 47, 138
Michaelis, Eli, 122
Moeser, Susan, v, 77, 97, 118, 137, 139
Morehead, John Motley, 2
Morehead Planetarium and Science Center, 129
Morehead Scholarship, 2

Napoleon, 91
National Merit Scholars, 53
National Research Center on Rural Education Support, 83
Naylor, Linda, 68
Nichol, Gene, 23, 65, 66, 75

INDEX

North Carolina Breast Cancer Screening Program, 58

Odum, Howard, 6, 12, 40, 65
Office of the Executive Vice Chancellor and Provost, 6
Office of General Counsel, 132
Office of Institutional Research, 70
Office of Technology Development, 133
Office of Undergraduate Research, 8, 52
Office of University Counsel, 68
Old Playmakers Theatre, 88
Old Well, 1
O'Malley, Michael, 106
Ort, Shirley, 54
Orthner, Dennis, 74

Partnership for Minority Advancement in the Biomolecular Sciences, 59
Partnership Program in Global Health, 98
Pelland, Kirk, 106
Perlman, Harvey, 121
Perry, David, 68, 99
Perry, Roger, 59, 137
Phillip Ambassadors Program, 98
Phillips, Earl "Phil", 98
Pisano, Etta, 17
Pit, The, 9
PlayMakers Repertory Company, 21, 88
Polk Place, 10, 36, 37
Program on Southern Politics, Media, and Public Life, 30

Quality Enhancement Plan, 94

Reed, Dan, 72, 99, 115
Reichart, Daniel, 94
Rice, Mabel, 122

Richardson, Dick, 3
Robinson, John Harvey, 87
Rogers, Mark, 122
Roosevelt, Franklin Delano, 65
Roper, Bill, 86
Runberg, Bruce, 20

Salmon, Ted, 93
Sanden, John Howard, 138
Sanford, Terry, 54
School of Dentistry, 64, 128
School of Education, 64, 83, 101
School of Government, 65
School of Law 23, 46, 54, 107
School of Medicine, 68, 114, 125
School of Pharmacy, 101
School of Public Health, 45, 58, 110
School of Social Work, 74
Schwab, Nelson, 85
Sells, Michael, 27, 28, 31
Seymore, Avon, 68
Sharp, Paul, 137
Shelton, Robert, 19, 22, 124, 133
Sitterson, Carlyle, 137, 138
Sitterson, Nancy, 3
Slain, Jonathan, 54
Smith, Mike, 65, 111
Sonja Haynes Stone Black Cultural Center, 24
South Building, 37
South Campus, 20
Spangler, Jr., C. D., 2
Spencer, Cornelia Phillips, 2, 10
Spray-Randleigh Fellowship, 71
Stravinsky, Igor, 139
Student Congress, 43
Student Government, 21
Summer Reading Program, 29, 31, 32, 36

Superfine, Richard, 18
Suttenfield, Nancy, 20

Task Force for a Better Workplace, 57, 63, 67
Task Force on Diversity, 73, 77, 84, 100
Task Force on Engagement, 77, 101
Task Force on Intellectual Climate, 8
Taylor, Elizabeth "Betsy," 68
Taylor, Nelson Ferebee, 2, 138
Taylor, Russ, 18
Thompson, Wanda, 106
Thorp, Holden, 17, 93, 137
Tomorrow Commission, 111
Traveling Education Science Laboratory, 59
Triangle National Lithography Center, 45
Tuition Advisory Task Force, 39, 85, 86

UNC Cancer Hospital, 128
UNC Health Care, 64, 96, 114
UNC Research Campus, 77, 81
University Cancer Research Fund, 107

Venable, Francis Preston, 2, 6
Venable Hall, 92

Waldrop, Tony, 19, 115, 124, 131, 132, 133
Washburn, Sean, 18
Wegner, Judith, 54, 70, 75, 87
White, Jesse, 65
William R. Kenan, Jr Charitable Trust, 89
Williams, Horace, 6, 19
Williams, "Stick," 59
Williford, Lynn, 100
Wilson Library, 45, 137, 138
Winston Residence Hall, 106
Wolfe, Thomas, 47
Wynn, Curtis, 65

Yarbrough, Marilyn, 43

Zhou, Otto, 18

JAMES MOESER was the ninth chancellor of the University of North Carolina at Chapel Hill. A native of Texas and trained as a concert organist, he earned bachelor's and master's degrees in music from the University of Texas at Austin and a doctorate from the University of Michigan. Formerly chancellor of the University of Nebraska-Lincoln, he began his work as chancellor at UNC on August 15, 2000. He established the Carolina Covenant and Carolina Performing Arts; led the $2.4 billion Carolina First campaign; oversaw a massive increase in research funding, including a major investment in genome research; and succeeded in increasing faculty salaries and greatly improving faculty retention. The physical campus was transformed by a $2.2 billion construction program that added six million net square feet of building space, while also adding twenty acres of green space. He currently resides in Chapel Hill with his wife, Susan.

www.ingramcontent.com/pod-product-compliance
Lightning Source LLC
Chambersburg PA
CBHW031147160426
43193CB00008B/284